For the past twenty years or so, I have been crossing and re-crossing the Antonine Wall several times a week. From office, airport or railway station, the route home takes me to the north side of Glasgow. The road curves, rises and falls—and before you know it, you are over the Antonine Wall.

I like to boast that I live on the *right* side of the Wall, the northern side, the part that the Romans left alone apart from sporadic punitive raids. But it's not immediately apparent to the casual traveller. Going home on the A879 (the Balmore Road, as we call it) there is just that inconspicuous swelling on the landscape you cross—too unremarkable to call it "tell-tale".

But a short detour takes in Bearsden, where there is a splendidly-preserved Roman bath-house which was excavated in the 1970s and is now open to the public, carefully laid out and maintained by the Historic Buildings and Monuments Directorate. It lies on the aptly-named Roman Road, and gives a vivid impression of the off-duty facilities provided for the soldiery who manned the Wall. Just a little to the east, on the way to Balmore, I can stop-off at New Kilpatrick Cemetery and study two short stretches of the stone base of the Wall.

Unlike Hadrian's Wall, which is so uncompromisingly (and profitably) visible, the Antonine Wall was built of stuff that for the most part has not endured. Also, it was built along the natural communications axis of central Scotland—so that succeeding generations of engineers and road-makers and commercial empire-builders have built along the same route, obliterating many traces of the Roman project.

But it hasn't all gone—far from it. And this welcome book by Anne Johnstone provides an invaluable guide for anyone who wants to explore the remains of the Wall.

Once you know where to look, there is plenty to see, and savour, and enjoy.

Magnus Magnusson

Chairman, ANCIENT MONUMENTS BOARD FOR SCOTLAND

Opposite: *The Wild Frontier at Bar Hill: The Antonine Wall strikes out across the Dunbartonshire countryside and detours round Castle Hill towards Croy.* ***Above:*** *Hutcheson Hill Distance Slab with the wild boar emblem of the Twentieth Legion.*

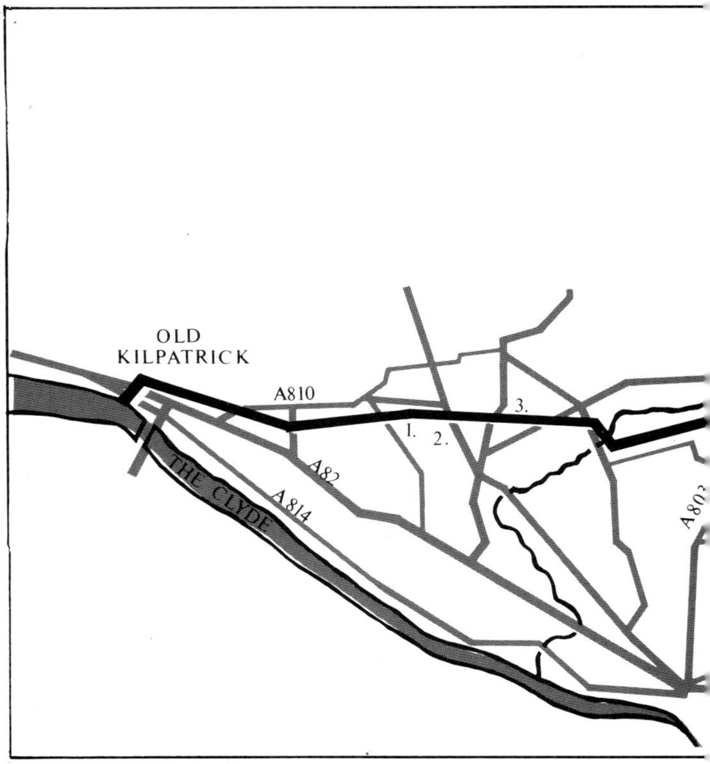

Around 142 AD, on the order of the Emperor Antoninus Pius, Roman soldiers set about slinging a military cordon across central Scotland from coast to coast.

It's not so far as it sounds, for, as the Roman writer Tacitus had observed picturesquely: "Clota (the Clyde) and Bodotria (the Forth), being carried so far inland by tides from opposite seas, are separated by but a narrow strip of land." In modern miles it's just 37, which makes it the narrowest part of Britain, a sort of raised waist.

The Antonine Wall, as it has become known, probably started at Bo'ness on the Forth and finished up at Old Kilpatrick on the Clyde, taking in the modern-day settlements of Falkirk, Castlecary, Croy, Twechar, Kirkintilloch, Bearsden and Duntocher.

The effect of the Wall was to bring the Lowlands of Scotland within the Roman Empire, taking over from Hadrian's Wall as Rome's north-west frontier. It was also intended to present to those living beyond it a physical and psychological barrier, a demonstration of military technology they could not hope to match.

More than 18 centuries later the Wall and the forts along its route are still the most striking evidence of the Roman occupation of Scotland. Even by modern standards it remains an impressive feat of engineering:

a stone base around 14-feet wide, slashed across by drainage culverts at regular intervals;
a superstructure, not of stone, but thin layers of turf stacked to a height of maybe ten feet;
a timber fence on top of the wall;
a 12-feet deep defensive ditch running along the north side of the wall;
a cobbled military road running parallel to the Wall on the south side;
a succession of forts of varying sizes incorporated into the rear of the Wall at approximately two-mile intervals.

This magnum opus must have filled the North Briton with a sense of helplessness. And a glimpse inside one of the 16 known forts along the frontier would have revealed a degree of sophistication completely beyond his ken. By contrast with his small, circular wooden huts within flimsy palisades, some of the forts were rectangular stone buildings with glasssed windows and red tiled roofs inside ramparts patrolled by sentries. Here was Roman society in miniature: soldiers playing board games, officers eating from fine Samian ware (the 2nd century equivalent of bone china), children running about the civilian settlements in elaborately styled leather shoes, carpenters and masons working in wood and stone, clerks compiling records to send back to Rome. Here a centrally heated bath-house; there, perhaps most curious of all, a flushing toilet!

Yet today while summer tourists queue to squeeze on to bits of Hadrian's Wall, only a handful of faithful pilgrims venture on to the Antonine frontier, let alone trace its full span between Forth and Clyde.

Of course, the Antonine Wall isn't so imposing a barrier as Hadrian's Wall, snaking across the Northumbrian Hills like a mini-Great Wall of China. But the Antonine barrier has a different charm, more discreet, more illusive.

It passes through that stratum of central Scotland irrevocably changed by the industrial revolution. So today it rubs shoulders with iron foundries and quarries and rubbish tips and fish meal factories. It is criss-crossed by motorways and railway lines and keeps on getting tangled up with the Forth and Clyde Canal. People drive golf balls along it and put electricity pylons on top of it. Here and there it disappears under people's kitchens and sitting rooms and herbacious borders.

Even in between all these distractions, the Wall is often hard to follow without a guide. Close on two millennia of exposure to the elements has reduced the superstructure to—at most—a little hump over the stone foundation. Frequently only the ditch, which shadowed the Wall to the north, remains visible and even that is often no more than a shallow groove across the landscape.

But it is part of the frontier's capacity to impress that just when you decide your pilgrimage is futile, it reveals a tantalising piece that has weathered the centuries remarkably well.

The Wild Frontier details several different Wall Walks taking in the best bits of the remains. The route is described from west to east because, generally speaking, the terrain gets more dramatic and exciting as Wall explorers travel east. This direction also retraces the steps of some of the Wall's earliest travellers. They include Major-General William Roy, founder father of the Ordnance Survey, who surveyed the Wall in 1755.

DIRECTIONS TO THE BEST BITS

The Clyde to Crow Hill

1. ***Castlehill:*** *the fort lies just south of Duntocher Road (A810) on the western outskirts of Bearsden. Park in*

Roger M Schlosser
1987
Edinburgh

THE WILD FRONTIER:
EXPLORING THE ANTONINE WALL
with
Anne Johnstone

CONTENTS

FOREWORD:
Magnus Magnusson

ACKNOWLEDGEMENTS
Particular thanks to Dr Lawrence Keppie, Keeper in Roman History at Glasgow University's Hunterian Museum and to Dr David Breeze, Inspector for the Historic Buildings and Monuments Section of the Scottish Development Department, for their useful comments and help with illustrations. The author also thanks Norman Hogg MP, John and Olive Cubbage, Geoff Bailey (Falkirk Museums Service), Sally Hunston, Alastair Balfour and June and Ian Johnstone. This volume grew from a series of features by the author which appeared in the Glasgow Herald in Spring 1985.

PHOTO CREDITS
Photographs on the following pages are reproduced by kind permission of:
Royal Commission on the Ancient and Historic Monuments of Scotland. 1, 2, 19, 27, 28, 29, 31, 33, 34, 35.
Hunterian Museum, University of Glasgow. 3, 7, 8, 12, 13, 15, 17, 23.
Anne Johnstone. 7, 9, 28, 29.
Nic Allen. 9, 10, 28, 29, 30, 31.
Mike Moore/David Breeze. 11, 25.
RMS. 27, 37.
William Cadell. 39.

BOOKS TO READ

Breeze D. J., *The Northern Frontier of Roman Britain,* 1982; *Roman Forts in Britain,* 1983. Cottrell L., *Seeing Roman Britain.* Revised edition 1967. Hanson W. and Maxwell G., *Rome's North-West Frontier,* 1983. Keppie L., *Roman Distance Slabs from the Antonine Wall,* 1979. Macdonald G., *The Roman Wall in Scotland.* Revised edition 1934. Robertson A., *The Antonine Wall.* New edition 1979. Skinner D., *The Countryside of the Antonine Wall,* 1973. Webster G., *The Roman Imperial Army of the First and Second Centuries AD.* Revised edition 1985. Ordnance Survey, *2½ inches-to-the-mile Map, The Antonine Wall,* 1969. HMSO leaflet, *The Antonine Wall.* 1974. SDD leaflet, *Bearsden Roman Bath-House.* Falkirk Museums, *The Roman Way: An Illustrated Explanatory Guide to the Antonine Wall in Falkirk District.* 1985.

Text: Anne Johnstone
Editor: Sheila Mackay
Production: Nic Allen
Advertising: Margaret Wilson
Design: Harriet Wylie
Printed in Scotland by
Alna Press Ltd., Broxburn

ISBN 0 948473 03 7

Published by MOUBRAY HOUSE PRESS
53 HIGH STREET, EDINBURGH EH1 1SR
Telephone: 031-556 4402

Antonine Road, where an Ancient Monuments sign indicates where the Wall crosses the road.

2. ***Bearsden Bath-House:*** *situated on the north side of Roman Road, Bearsden, near junction with Grange Road. Park in car park on Rowan Road by Post Office. By rail: take the Glasgow suburban service to Hillfoot [on the Milngavie line], cross the main road outside the exit and follow Roman Drive. It turns into Roman Road [5-10 minute walk].*

3. ***New Kilpatrick Cemetery:*** *two lengths of the stone base of the rampart are exposed here. The cemetery is on the north side of Boclair Road (B8049), half-a-mile east of its junction with Milngavie Road (A81). By rail: to Hillfoot [see above], then walk south down Milngavie Road for 100 yards and turn left into Boclair Road [10-15 minute walk].*

Balmuildy to Bar Hill

4. ***Bar Hill:*** *the fort lies up a hill half-a-mile east of Twechar village. Take the turning into Twechar off the Auchendavy to Auchinstarry road (B8023), which follows the Forth and Clyde Canal. A few yards down the turning, near the War Memorial, take the rough track on the left to Bar Farm, marked by an Ancient Monuments sign. Those with delicate cars may prefer to walk.*

Croy to Falkirk

5. ***Croy Hill:*** *the fort is up a steep hill a third of a mile east of Croy village. Take the Kilsyth to Cumbernauld road (B802) and park beside the Old Duke public house. Access to the path is via the lorry park adjacent. Good walk from here through to Castlecary?*

6. ***Castlecary:*** *the fort lies just east of the A80 Glasgow-Stirling dual carriageway, in a field crossed by the Glasgow-Edinburgh railway line. You can cross the A80 on the Castlecary to Bonnybridge road (B816), then take the little side road to the right, marked Walton. The fort is opposite a bungalow aptly named "Castra".*

7. ***Seabegs Wood:*** *good stretch of ditch and best example of the Military Way. The wood lies between Castlecary and Bonnybridge on the south side of the B816. Park in the car park at the eastern end of the village of Allendale or beside the road at the eastern end of the wood, where there is space for two or three cars.*

8. ***Rough Castle:*** *the fort is to be found about one mile east of the town of Bonnybridge up a side road which progressively deteriorates. Access is off the B816 near the former Smith and Wellstood factory with its distinctive mural, just south of the canal. Drivers should take a new access road, marked by a row of saplings about 50 yards south of the foundry. Go straight over the little railway bridge after Airlock Double Glazing. Follow single track road for ¼-mile, then turn left through gate, over cattle-grid and follow track to car park.*

9. ***Watling Lodge:*** *best example of the Antonine ditch. It lies on the south side of Tamfourhill Road, which links Falkirk with High Bonnybridge. If coming from Falkirk turn left of Camelon Road (A803) into Glenfuir Road at Rosebank Distillery. Turn right into Tamfourhill Road at Barr's soft drinks factory. Parking available in industrial estate on the north side of the road or on road itself.*

Falkirk to the Forth

10. ***Callendar Park:*** *good stretch of Wall and ditch. Turn south from Callendar Road (A803) into Estate Avenue and park in car park at far end. Walk back up Estate Avenue a few yards and take footpath to the right in front of tower block (Leishman Tower), marked by Ancient Monuments sign. By rail: train to Falkirk High Station [on the half-hour from Glasgow and Edinburgh]. Walk down High Station Road. Take first right into Glen Brae, then first left into Kemper Avenue. The Antonine ditch crosses the south edge of the Kemper Avenue Car Park and goes behind tower block [Eastburn Tower]. Thence follow signs [10-15 minute walk].*

11. ***Polmonthill:*** *good stretch of the ditch. It lies just south of the Bo'ness to Polmont Road (A and B904). Best view is to be had by turning south off B904 up side road marked Inveravon and Upper Kinneil. Stop by the gas sub-station and look west across the River Avon. The Wall itself is covered by a plastic ski-slope. The ditch is the distinctive groove beside it.*

12. ***Kinneil Park:*** *consolidated remains of a fortlet, in the western outskirts of Bo'ness. Turn left off Dean Road (A904) into Provost Road then right into Deangate Gardens and left across a bridge leading into Kinneil Estate. The fortlet lies between two ponds several hundred yards west of car park at Kinneil House.*

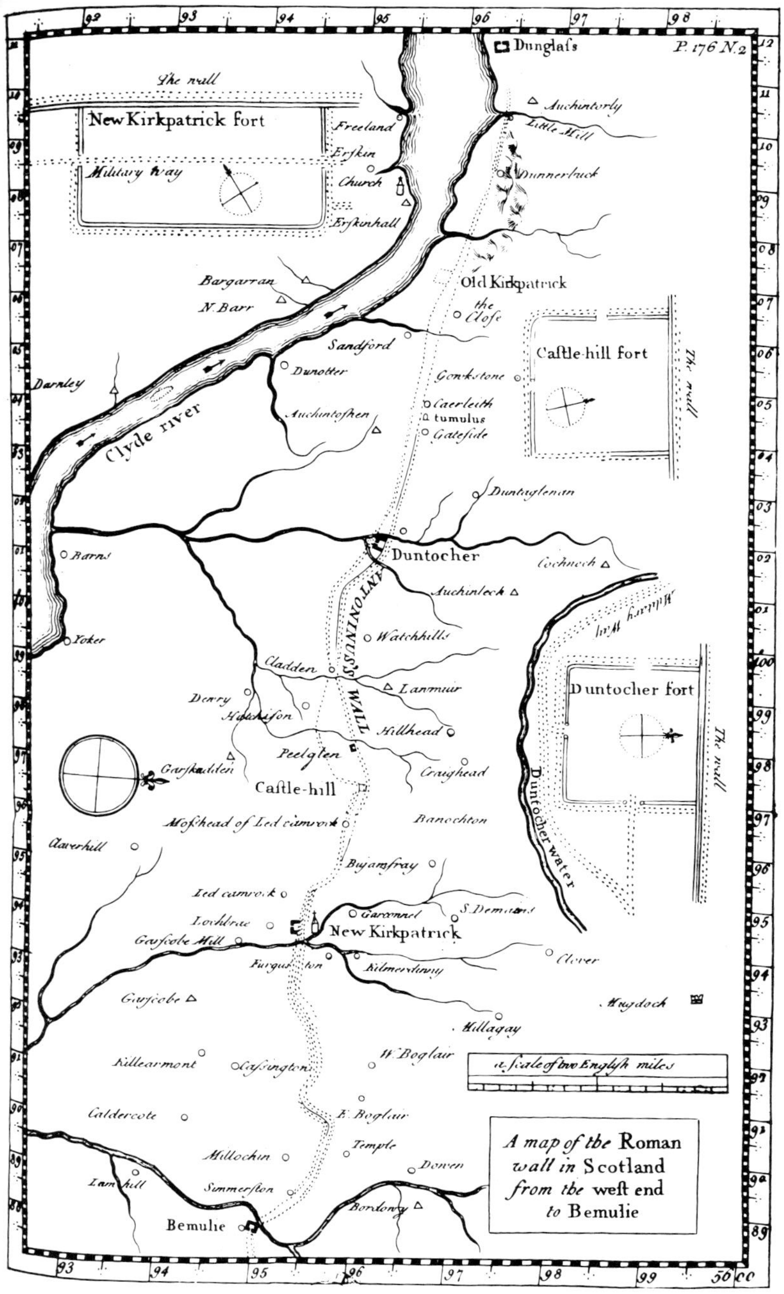

EXPLORING THE WALL

THE CLYDE TO CROW HILL

It is around 2000 years since the Roman army, that extraordinarily successful military machine, struck out from a city state to engulf the known world like a tide. By the mid-second century its Empire was like a great blanket of Roman rule stretching from the mouth of the Danube, down to the Gulf of Aqaba, across to the sands of the Sahara and north through Britain to the Clyde estuary.

Yet how many of those who walk their dogs and ride their bikes along the Forth and Clyde Canal towpath at Old Kilpatrick realise that this was the north-west corner of the Roman Empire? And how many know that when the Romans decided to build a great wall across Scotland in 142 AD this is where they finished?

Today Old Kilpatrick is dwarfed by the structurally troublesome span of the Erskine Bridge and, a few street names apart, exhibits little sense of history. They say you can see the Great Wall of China from the moon. Yet you can stand right on top of where the Antonine Wall reached the Clyde and all you can see along the line of it is the SMT bus depot.

You can try looking downstream and imagining Roman galleys, laden with amphoras of wine and olive oil to supply the Wall garrison, pulling into a Roman port, now lost in the mud, but the view is obscured by the Esso terminal at Bowling and tankers full of petrol from Fawley refinery.

But there is one little link with the past here. Beside a quaint little opening bridge across the canal is Ferrydyke Cottage where in 1790, during the construction of the canal, workmen accidentally uncovered a Roman bath-house. And at least a century before that a carved stone slab had been found near the same spot. It's in the Hunterian Museum at Glasgow University now and is almost certainly the 'terminal' slab mounted on the Wall by the soldiers of the Twentieth Legion who completed the final stretch.

It shows the goddess Victory, topless and reclining nonchalantly, with a palm frond in one hand and a congratulatory wreath in the other. "It's all over, we've won," the slab seems to say. Strange to think the Romans would withdraw to the Hadrian line within a few years.

The bus depot looks rather impenetrable, so perhaps it's best to head next for Gavinburn Gardens, a neat cul-de-sac of semis, built in the 1920s. The bath-house at Ferrydyke turned out to be in an annexe of a fort, part of which lies under some of the gardens. One resident is definitely not a keen gardener and when he's told about the Roman fort, his eyes light up. "You can tell they archaeologists, they can come and dig my garden any time," he says.

Another is similarly taken aback by the idea that the headquarters building for the fort probably lies under his rosebed and you half-wonder if he'll rush out with a spade the moment you've closed the gate.

Roman bits and pieces are still turning up here. In 1969 workmen digging an inspection pit for the now defunct Weir's garage nearby, pulled out a beautiful altar dedicated to Jove.

The next stretch of the Wall line is cut first by the Helensburgh railway line, then by four lines of traffic, thundering up and down the A82. But you can pick up the route on the western outskirts of Duntocher at Carleith Farm, though there's nothing to see. It follows Beeches Road, where neat modern boxes with Korean Hardwood doors and freshly washed cars outside, give way to grey run-down council houses.

Descending to the site of the Roman bridge which once crossed the Duntocher Burn, there's the Antonine Sports Centre, like a great affirmation of an engagingly loony idea. It's hard to miss as the name is splashed along the side in yard-high yellow letters.

The friendly steward points out some "Antonine rocks" halfway up the hill in Goldenhill Park

Maps by John Horsley from "Britannia Romana", 1732, appear throughout "The Wild Frontier". They are remarkably accurate, but modern-day Wall explorers might also follow the Ordnance Survey map of the Antonine Wall.

beyond and sure enough, there's a short stretch of Wall base exposed behind a high spiked fence. It's the first bit of Wall to be seen but it's hard to get excited about this sad square of stones.

On the summit of the hill the Romans had built a tiny fortlet, 60 feet square. Though this was later expanded to make a proper fort, it's still the smallest on the Wall. The most charming find from this site was a statuette of a stout, rather Picasso-like water nymph holding a shell over her tummy with a hole for water to cascade from. It's in the Hunterian Museum now and the only clue to the Roman connection on the site is a neat little "Roman Garden", trimmed with laurel bushes.

Then it's down past the Raj Mahal restaurant and the car dealer and up Cleddens Road, past two archaeologically productive farms. In 1812, an exquisite stone slab was found at Braidfield Farm. It shows four figures, including two winged girls with top knots holding up a sign saying: "For the Emperor Caesar Titus Aelius Hadrianus Antoninus Augustus, Father of his Country, a detachment of the Sixth Victorious, Loyal and Faithful Legion completed the rampart work over 3240 feet."

And at Cleddens Farm up the road, a passer-by in the 1970s found another slab, erected by men from the Twentieth Legion. It had been ploughed up, propped against a byre and forgotten. And whoever had whitewashed the barn had diligently whitewashed the slab as well. It took ages to get it off at the Hunterian Museum.

In a flat field covered with old bits of farm machinery and household rubbish beside the farm, Dr Lawrence Keppie of Glasgow University discovered a fortlet in 1977. "I chose the site because it afforded such a good view of the two adjoining forts at Goldenhill and Castlehill and it turned out to be spot on," he says, making the process sound deceptively easy.

To The Bath-House At Bearsden

The bleak protuberance of Drumchapel comes into view as you head off between low hills and down to a scruffy burn. Though the woods round here look pretty scrappy and there's lots of litter, they are very old. In fact, they may even pre-date the Romans. There are plans to clean up the area and turn it into a nature reserve.

The ditch, which ran parallel to the Wall, is easy to follow here because there's a hedge planted in it. It leads up to the summit of Castlehill where dreary Drumchapel gives way to neat Bearsden.

Old accounts describe a fort on Castlehill but it's never been excavated because, with admirable restraint, archaeologists have agreed to leave it for future generations with more refined techniques.

Above left: *Author Anne Johnstone with David Breeze at New Kilpatrick Cemetery.* ***Above right:*** *Picasso-like Water Nymph found at Duntocher, now in Glasgow's Hunterian Museum.*

ANTONINUS WHO?

Despite his long reign (138–161 AD), we know remarkably little about the man who gave his name to the Wall, the Roman Emperor Antoninus Pius. He was the adopted son of the previous Emperor, Hadrian, and may have been a stop-gap choice, intended to fill in until the young Marcus Aurelius came of age. Having distinguished himself as a proconsul in Asia, he was an administrator rather than a military man and, according to the contemporary Greek writer Pausanias, he "never willingly made war".

And yet the very first thing he did on coming to power was to initiate the re-occupation of southern Scotland and, according to his biographer: "after driving back the barbarians, built another wall, this time of turf."

A number of reasons have been given for this apparently uncharacteristic initiative. The suppression of a revolt by tribesmen in the Scottish Lowlands? A sweetener for the hawks in the military high command in Rome? The economic advantages of acquiring the fertile, well-drained areas of land in southern Scotland?

Whatever the reason, the conquest was swift. Around the end of 142 AD Antoninus received the accolade *Imperator*, or victorious commander-in-chief, celebrated on a series of specially minted coins proclaiming the subjugation of Britain. And it didn't seem to matter that Antoninus never came to Britain and wasn't personally involved in the fighting because, as Emperor, the glory was his.

The death of Antoninus seems to have marked the end of an era. His successor, Marcus Aurelius, was soon facing serious military threats from the Rhine and the eastern Mediterranean, as well as northern Britain. In the resultant damage limitation exercise, he probably saw withdrawal from southern Scotland as the least painful option. The order to retreat may have been as soon as 164 AD.

If these calculations are correct, the Antonine Wall marked Rome's north-west frontier for barely 20 years. We must picture the garrison grimly dismantling the buildings and carefully burying the Distance Slabs to avert the indignity of vandalism. Then, loading what they could on to carts, they headed south down Dere Street to refortify Hadrian's Wall, rehanging the gates which had been complacently removed from the forts and milecastles and cleaning out the ditch. Later the Wall itself would be strengthened and partly rebuilt. This time there would be no going back■

The other sure sign there's a fort there, apart from the terrific views in every direction, is that when winter gales uproot the beech trees on its summit, Roman pottery can be found entwined in their roots.

Then it's down past Castlehill Farm with its flock of geese (a suitably Roman security system), across Antonine Road and on down the path, between modern houses, which marks the line of the Wall.

Two bits of the Wall's base have been exposed in this bit of suburbia: one is in Roman Park, behind Mulverton Avenue, and the other is in a garden in Thorn Road. Its owner came upon it accidentally in 1973 and decided to turn it into a rockery.

A little further on, in Roman Road, Bearsden, there's a bath-house which is probably the best thing to see on the whole line of the Wall. It was located by Dr David Breeze, one of the Inspectors of Ancient Monuments in 1973 and has since been laid out for public inspection, with an excellent information panel showing a reconstruction.

If you imagine that Ancient Monuments inspectors wear uniforms and peaked caps and frown on any kind of naughtiness, then you're in for a surprise. Dr Breeze, the inspector in charge of the Wall, wears a scruffy green waterproof and a rather mischievous grin. He has that uncanny knack of bringing heaps of stones alive.

Roman bath-houses vary quite a bit in basic design. This one is a classic example and an impressive reminder of the importance attached to basic hygiene, even on this far flung frontier of the Empire. Apart from the wooden changing room, the complex is made of stone with cavity walls and underfloor heating. There's a series of rooms ranging from cold to hot, plus hot and cold baths.

It's generally assumed that bath-houses were used for other off-duty leisure activities, like playing dice and board games. Dr Breeze is sceptical about this: "Everyone says these bath-houses were the Roman equivalent of the NAAFI but we've got to look carefully at the evidence." He believes the head of Fortuna (the Romans' Lady Luck), which he found in the cold bath, was probably nothing to do with the playing of games of chance. "She was intended to protect the men when they were in their most defenceless state," he says, with a grin.

Analysis of sewage deposits from here shows that the diet of a soldier garrisoned on the Wall included wheat, barley, coriander, poppy seeds, figs, raspberries, strawberries, wild celery and hazel nuts. Scientists at Glasgow University have been doing further research to determine the cholesterol level in the diet.

"The balance seems closer to a modern vegetarian diet than a carnivorous or omnivorous one. The staple diet was probably some sort of porridge or gruel, some of which must have been infested because we've found traces of grain beetles in the samples," says Dr Breeze.

This may not seem much of an appetizer for lunch but peckish pilgrims can grab a bite at Bearsden's modern bath-house, the Allander Sports Centre (non-members pay 20p to get in). Alternatively, there's the cafe at Hillfoot, which has a justifiable reputation for its ice cream.

Top: *Anne Johnstone with pupils of Castlehill Primary School re-enacting frontier times at the Bearsden Roman Bath-house.* ***Above:*** *A view of the Bearsden Bath-house today.*

View From The Hill
Next stop is in New Kilpatrick Cemetery on Boclair Road. If cemeteries can be beautiful, this one is. Everything about it is impeccably neat and clean, including the two sections of Wall base left exposed among the tombstones. Note the drainage culverts. In front of one of these exposed areas there's a sort of lawn and it comes as a bit of a shock to discover that this is the paupers' graveyard, where those without means or relatives to pay the expenses, are buried in unmarked graves. It may sound Victorian but it still happens.

Robert Philp, the superintendent, is bursting with pride in his cemetery. "I'm pretty strict but I have to be. Leave that grass a couple of days and it's impossible to get back. A lot of people come here just for the walk, you know. I don't mind that. I want people to enjoy my cemetery but I don't want folk playing football all over people's departed relatives. Internment is our first priority."

It's not surprising people come here for walks. The view from the top of the rise is breathtakingly panoramic, north to the Campsies and the mouth of the Blane Valley, west across Bearsden to tree-topped Castlehill and east across the central belt towards Kilsyth.

From here the Wall crosses a corner of Douglas Park Golf Course, where the line of the ditch is clearly visible but across the other side of Boclair Road it disappears, ploughed out over generations. Following the line marked on the Ordnance Survey map leads you to Crow Hill which looks like the perfect site for a fortlet but nobody has ever found one.

There is a great view from here but if your sights are set on a cuppa, there's one to be had among the potplants at the Findlay Clark Garden Centre just over the hill.

BUILDING THE WALL

Roman soldiers were never allowed to rest on their laurels. No sooner had they subjugated a new area to Roman rule than they would put down their swords and javelins and take up picks and shovels. Roman prowess in battle was easily matched by building and engineering skills—those long straight roads, well-defended forts with buildings of stone and wood and the great ramparts they threw across the countryside to give the Empire a nice neat edge.

All around its fringes in the 2nd century, massive building projects were in hand. Archaeologists, following the footsteps of the Imperial Army at a distance of some 2,000 years, have unearthed many of its tools—shovels, pickaxes, turf cutters, plumb bobs, masons' hammers and literally millions of nails. Though the frontier would ultimately be garrisoned by auxiliary troops, non-citizens recruited from the border provinces, the construction work was done by the legionaries, Roman citizens from long established provinces who formed the backbone of the Roman army. Each legion would have its own masons, blacksmiths, carpenters and other specialist craftsmen.

Perhaps the most eloquent tribute to legionary labour came from the Emperor Hadrian, who inspected a wall building operation by the Third Legion in North Africa. His description survives in an inscription:

> "The building of fortifications, which others would have spread over several days, you completed in a single day: a wall requiring much labour and of a type which is normally built for a permanent winter camp, you constructed in no greater time than it takes to build one of turf which, being cut in pieces of equal size is both carried and handled with ease, so built up without trouble as being by its own nature pliable and level; you built your wall with heavy uneven stones, you dug a trench in a straight line in hard gravel and trimmed it smooth. When this work had been approved, you went into the camp, hurriedly ate a meal, sprang to arms and followed the cavalry out"—presumably to a military exercise.

A generation later and on the north-westerly fringes of the Empire, another group of legionaries

***Above:** The base of the Antonine Wall at New Kilpatrick Cemetery. **Opposite:** Reconstruction drawing by M. Moore of the building of the Antonine Wall, showing the stone base, turfing and wooden palisades.*

was involved in a similar gruelling task. There were three legions garrisoned in Britain for most of the Roman occupation and all of them had a hand in building the Antonine Wall, together with its military road, defensive ditch and the forts and fortlets strung along its length.

Unanswered Questions

Historians are still arguing about why the Wall was built at all, so soon after the laborious completion of the Hadrian frontier, 73 miles long and all in stone.

In the late first century, Agricola, Britain's best known Roman governor, had fought a number of successful campaigns in Scotland, establishing a route between the Forth and the Tay and defeating a Caledonian army on the slopes of Mons Graupius (probably somewhere near the Moray Firth). But thereafter Roman policy was directed not to bringing the northern tribes into the Roman Empire but keeping them out.

So what was Antoninus playing at? Was the new Emperor simply seeking to appease the "hawks" in the military high command? Or was it because of fighting in southern Scotland between pro- and anti- Roman tribes? Maybe a bit of both.

And why, and exactly when, was the Antonine Wall evacuated? To complicate matters further, the Wall seems to have been deserted twice: once briefly during the 150s and again permanently in the next decade. These evacuations were not necessarily the result of the Wall being stormed by hostile troops from the north. In fact, the most popular theory is that the withdrawals were necessitated by shortages of manpower elsewhere in the Empire.

And what was the Wall for exactly? Was it a defensive line, a sort of fighting platform? Or was it simply an administrative barrier, designed to give a neat edge to the Roman Empire and keep an eye on movements on both sides of the Wall?

Legionary Labour

The lion's share of Wall work seems to have gone to the Second Legion, normally headquartered in Caerleon in South Wales. Probably the full legion of over 5,000 men worked on the new frontier. Smaller detachments of perhaps 1,000 to 2,000 from the Sixth and Twentieth Legions, based in York and Chester respectively, were also involved. While building work was in progress they would have lived in temporary camps nearby. Invisible today at ground level, a number of these camps are clearly visible from the air, where they stand out as dark rectangles with rounded corners, like giant playing cards. Specific information about which legion worked where along the Wall is provided by the Distance Slabs set up to commemorate the completion of particular lengths of the rampart by a particular legion.

The wall builders must have been preceded on the scene by surveyors who decided the exact route the Wall was to take across Lowland Scotland. For obvious tactical reasons the Antonine surveyors chose to site most of the Wall on north-facing slopes, following the south sides of the Kelvin and Carron Valleys with a breathtaking view north to the Campsie fells and Kilsyth Hills. It is worth noting that they chose such a direct route that much of it was imitated by the builders of both the Forth and Clyde Canal and the Glasgow-Edinburgh railway line. Only in the west, where north-facing slopes were not available, does the Wall seem to lose its way, hopping from one hillock to the next.

The term "murus cespiticius" (turf wall) to describe the Antonine frontier is a little misleading. In fact the Wall is constructed on a stone base, usually 14 feet wide and pierced by culverts at regular intervals. Most of it is rough cobbles but with kerbs of dressed stones on either side. It was an arrangement which gave the Wall structural stability and ensured that it was well-drained. Several pieces of the Wall base have been left exposed. By far the best are the two sections in New Kilpatrick Cemetery, in Boclair Road, Bearsden.

The main superstructure is turf blocks, probably originally piled to a height of 9 or 10 feet and tapering towards the top. There has been a lot of argument about how it was finished off. Some authorities reckon there was a walkway along the top, covered by wooden duckboards, with a little fence on the north side, bringing the total height of the rampart to about 14 feet. Others say there is no evidence of this and, besides, the Wall was never meant to be patrolled in the style of a medieval rampart. Eighteen centuries of pressure and decay have reduced the Wall to at most a low hump. So today it is less impressive than the V-shaped defensive ditch which runs parallel to it a few yards to the north. Though some sections, notably Watling Lodge on the western edge of Falkirk, still present an imposing obstacle.

The third continuous element of the frontier is a road, the Military Way, which lay around 40 yards south of the Wall. About 16 feet wide and cambered so that rainwater would drain off, it provided a quick means of communication and transport along the frontier. Though now grassed over, the best surviving stretch is in Seabegs Wood west of Bonnybridge.

How long did it take to build the Antonine frontier? The number of variables involved in the Antonine Wall makes the calculation pretty hypothetical. But historian Gordon Maxwell has made a brave attempt to come up with 1,730,000 "man days"!

Incidentally, he reckons the Wall consumed 950 acres of turf, 52,000 cubic yards of stone and one million cubic feet of timber. His "man days" calculation makes an allowance for the construction of fortlets, like the one on display in Kinneil Park. These are virtually identical to the milecastles on Hadrian's Wall, which, as their name implies, occurred every Roman mile (1,618 yards). Only nine have so far been discovered along the Antonine Wall (length 41 Roman miles), though there could be more.

However, Maxwell's calculation does not include time taken on building the forts themselves, another task traditionally assigned to Roman legionaries, Several dedication slabs have been retrieved from forts on the Wall showing that the legions were involved in this work. The Antonine Wall forts have long puzzled historians. There are a lot of them—at least 16, compared with 17 for Hadrian's Wall, which is nearly double its length. They vary considerably in size from Mumrills (6.5 acres) to tiny Duntocher (.5 acre). And it is obvious from their construction that some were built before the Wall and others after. Some are very close to fortlets, which you would think would be fairly evenly spaced between forts, to plug the gaps.

Another historian, John Gillam, has come up with rather an ingenious explanation for all these forts and fortlets which clutter the Antonine frontier. He believes that the original blueprint envisaged just six major forts on the Wall, interspersed by fortlets every mile, just like on Hadrian's. The six were Old Kilpatrick and Carriden at the two ends and Balmuildy, Bar Hill, Castlecary and Mumrills in between. These were built first. However, at some point there was a change of plan and a lot of additional forts were added in. Why remains a mystery. Renewal of hostilities in the localty perhaps?

Using the Gillam theory, Maxwell also makes a stab at the timetable for building the Antonine frontier. He reckons the work began in 142 AD and, including the building of the extra forts, ended in late 144 AD with a mad dash to the Clyde before the onset of winter.

Spilling The Secrets

While debate rages on about unanswered questions, a century of scholarship has gone a long way towards making the mute remains of the Antonine frontier spill their secrets.

Aerial photography has revealed a number of "fortlets", plugging gaps between forts on the Wall and a number of rectangular enclosures just back from the line of the Wall. They probably housed squads of legionaries during the construction phase.

Most productive of all have been the dozens of excavations stretching back to those carried out in

Left: *Tools of the Wall builders, now in the Hunterian Museum.*

the 1890s under the aegis of the Glasgow Archaeological Society.

These digs have provided not just detailed information about how the Wall and its forts were constructed but also knowledge of every aspect of the lives of its occupying force from the gods they worshipped to what they ate for breakfast.

Perhaps most revealing have been the inscribed stone slabs erected by construction squads to mark the completion of a fort building or a stretch of Wall. These slabs, many now in the Hunterian Museum at Glasgow Univesity, imbue this piece of military technology with a touchingly human face. The so-called Distance Slabs record not just the legions from which the work squads were drawn (the Second, Sixth and Twentieth), but also how much of the Wall they built. Many also depict motifs and scenes evidently designed to leave the beholder in no doubt of the power of Rome.

Modern-Day Garrison

After the final Roman withdrawal, the Wall and its installations were not razed to the ground by vengeful tribesmen, who had resented this military cordon cutting through their land. Instead, they offered the greater insult of simple neglect. And so the frontier had lain abandoned and largely forgotten for 18 centuries. The most serious threats to its remains have been the ravages of industrial development and suburban sprawl during the past 200 years.

Now, thankfully, that process has been halted by protective legislation. Just about all of the Wall, or the line where it once ran, are Scheduled Ancient Monuments, except the bits that have been obliterated by modern urban development. That means owners have to inform the Scottish Office if they want to alter or damage it in any way and the Secretary of State or local council may say they cannot.

On top of that, about four and a half miles of the Wall have the special protection of a guardianship agreement. This involves a form of contract between the owner and the Secretary of State. These bits are maintained by a permanent squad who form the Wall's modern-day garrison, protecting it against not hostile tribes but vandals, litter bugs and encroaching wilderness.

Above: *Trajan's Column in Rome is a unique historical document showing legionaries constructing a rampart. It is a scene of frenetic activity. Each man, muscle-bound and literally fighting fit, is engaged in his own task; some cut logs, some are doing carpentry, some are carving out blocks of turf, while others are digging a ditch and filling baskets with earth. In the background a rampart is under construction.*

THE DISTANCE SLABS

Whenever a squad of Roman legionaries completed a sector of the Antonine Wall, it was permitted the modest reward of erecting carved stone slabs giving details of its achievement. Eighteen such slabs have survived and two more are known about—one was destroyed in a fire and another has disappeared. Taken together they represent a quite remarkable body of evidence about the Romans' world. They tell us about their ceremonies, their gods, their emblems, their clothes, their architecture and the skills of their craftsmen. Most of all they help us understand how the Romans perceived themselves and their enemies. Nothing quite like them has been found anywhere else in the Roman world.

Nearly all the slabs are in Glasgow University's Hunterian Museum. Exceptions are the Bridgeness Slab, which had marked the eastern terminus of the rampart, now to be found in the Royal Museum of Scotland in Edinburgh's Queen Street, and a rather worn one in Glasgow's municipal art gallery at Kelvingrove.

They are not like the dull plaques we use today to adorn our buildings and public works, for the legionary stonemasons embellished their work with elaborate borders, often incorporating the figures of gods and goddesses, men and animals. These slabs were not merely a bald record of the job just completed but an important part of the Roman propaganda machine. Like the Wall itself, they were intended to reinforce in the native beholder a sense of being hopelessly outclassed.

Because the Romans appear to have made efforts to conceal the slabs by burying them when they retreated from the Wall, some are in remarkably good state of preservation. Most of them have small dovetail cramp holes, which would have been used to attach them to a backing, probably the Wall itself. Though the sandstone slabs are now yellowish or grey in appearance, traces of red paint found on some of them indicate that originally they might have been brightly decorated.

From the 20 slabs that have been rediscovered we know that each completed sector was marked at either end by at least one slab and possibly two, one on either side of the Wall. On that basis there could be as many as 60 slabs. Though some will have been destroyed, some still must lie buried under the houses, gardens, fields and factories near the line of the wall, just waiting to be unearthed.

The scenes depicted on the Distance Slabs contain a great deal of information about the construction of the Antonine Wall. Virtually all the slabs refer to Antoninus Pius, confirming that this is the "turf wall" described by a contemporary chronicler. Most of them give him his full set of names—"Imperator Caesar Titus Aelius Hadrianus Antoninus Augustus Pius, father of his Country". The slabs confirm that the Wall was built by all three legions stationed in Britain at the time: the Second, the Sixth and the Twentieth. On the slabs they use their full titles, "II Augusta", "VI Victrix" and "XX Valeria Victrix", usually abbreviated to "Aug", "Vic" and "VV". In addition, slabs of the Second and Twentieth Legions often bear their legionary emblem—a Capricorn or Pegasus for the Second and a wild boar for the Twentieth.

The Distance Slabs can be found at the Hunterian Museum. ***Top:*** *Summerston Slab found near Balmuildy, II Legion.* ***Centre left:*** *Slab depicting the Goddess Victory, Old Kilpatrick, XX Legion.* ***Centre right:*** *Hutcheson Hill Slab, XX Legion.* ***Below left:*** *Braidfoot Slab, Duntocher, VI Legion.* ***Below right:*** *Duntocher Slab, II Legion.*

Collecting the slabs has been a long and difficult process. Those who found them often did not realise their significance. Some were built into the walls of houses for decoration. Others were simply abandoned. The core of the collection was brought together by William Dunlop, principal of Glasgow University between 1694 and 1700.

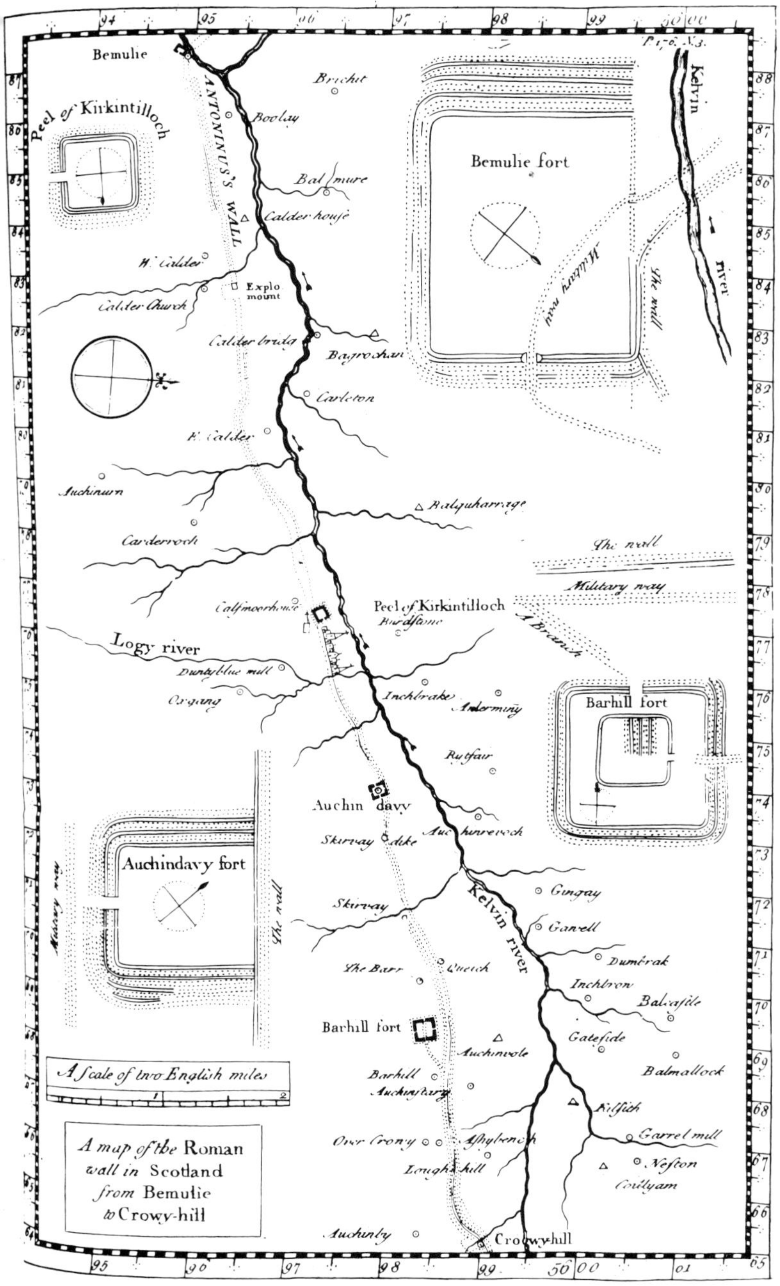

EXPLORING THE WALL

BALMUILDY TO BAR HILL

Of the thousands of Glasgow-bound commuters who flood into Lambhill on the Balmore Road each morning, few can realise they are driving across the corner of a Roman fort.

And Balmuildy, set in a field just south of the River Kelvin, is no ordinary fort either. It is one of only two stone-walled forts on the Antonine Wall and, with its impressive north gate, may have marked a special frontier station for those wishing to enter the Roman Empire.

It was Balmuildy too, in 1698, that provided definite proof that this was indeed the "second wall" which the biographer of Emperor Antoninus Pius had referred to. A fragment of Roman inscription was discovered which mentions work done by the Second Legion for Lollius Urbicus, the Governor of Britain who was responsible for building the Antonine Wall.

Jewel of Antiquity, Cupids and Canal

Alexander Gordon, an 18th-century antiquarian, who walked the Wall around 1725, and was somewhat prone to exaggeration, called this stone "the most invaluable Jewel of Antiquity that ever was found in the Island of Britain." It certainly settled a few arguments because before the Balmuildy Stone was unearthed, some authors thought this "second wall" was between the Tyne and the Solway Firth, just like Hadrian's.

Balmuildy Fort is also the source of a delightful statuette of Mars, God of War, with shield and javelin and little Gorgon heads on his knees, intended to literally petrify anyone daring to look. You'll find him in the Hunterian Museum.

Excavation on the site uncovered some quite sophisticated commanding officer's quarters, with all the mod cons a Roman gentleman would have been used to. These included rooms heated by hypocausts (a sort of underfloor central heating) and a toilet flushed by rainwater.

Today there's little to be seen at Balmuildy, though, stranded on a drawing board, there's a plan to turn Wester Balmuildy Farm into a visitor centre and expose some of the ruins.

East along the back of Bishopbriggs, the line of the Roman frontier follows the road, past the Centurion Brickworks and on through a scrappy no-man's land between city and country. Maps always make it look as if there's a definite line between town and country, but look anywhere just beyond the suburban sprawl and you find a band of peri-urban squalor.

The woodland on the right is Wilderness Plantation which was first planted way back in the 1780s. "Note the interesting ground flora," the man from the Nature Conservancy Council had said, but the amateur eye has difficulty getting past the dense undergrowth of litter.

Part of the Wall here has disappeared through quarrying. Now the resultant hole is what we're meant to call an "amenity site", in other words a rubbish tip, and there's a white cloud of screaming seagulls hovering overhead.

Next the Wall goes straight through the 10th, 17th and 2nd holes of Cawdor Golf Course, though it's a good idea to get permission from the very obliging club staff before traipsing across.

The course has been restructured at a cost of £100,000, mostly fruit machine money and looks good enough to eat off. It may sound unorthodox, especially for female travellers, but it's worth trying to get a peek into the men's locker room in the stately 17th-century clubhouse. That's because there's a charming little Roman dedication slab there, showing two naked cupids holding up a wreath with "Second Legion" inscribed inside.

The house once belonged to the Stirling family (motto: Gang Forward) and the slab was apparently a gift from John Napier, the inventor of logarithms, who married into the family. It's thought to have originated from Auchendavy, the fort on the other side of Kirkintilloch, and must have come from a building constructed by the Second Legion.

Also dominating the dining room there's a

modern mural of a Roman centurion, once identified by Andy Cameron, after a particularly gruelling Pro-Am, as "the last chap never to lose a golf ball on this course".

The line of the Wall continues into the smaller adjoining Keir course then emerges by a sharp bend in the Forth and Clyde Canal, opposite the site of Cadder Fort. It was excavated in the 1930s, in advance of its complete destruction by sand quarrying.

Quarrying has been one of the greatest modern enemies of the Wall, though all the surviving bits are now protected by planning legislation and guardianship agreements.

In the 18th century the chief destroyer of the Wall was the Forth and Clyde Canal, built between 1767 and 1790 with money from the forfeited estates of Jacobite supporters. Along much of their lengths Wall and Canal run side by side and between Cadder and the village of Twechar, five miles to the east, they intersect no fewer than five times.

While the Wall goes straight from Cadder to Glasgow Bridge, along the distinctively straight road to Kirkintilloch, the Canal takes a leisurely detour. This stretch has been cleared of weeds and rubbish by the Forth and Clyde Canal Society, and in summer three ferry boats ply its waters, including the old Govan Ferry. The stables, which once housed the horses that drew industrial barges along the canal, have recently undergone an impressive transformation into a hostelry, which serves lunchtime meals.

It's a pity Kirkintilloch hasn't produced more concrete evidence of the Roman occupation because the folk there are very interested in local history and the charming Little Auld Kirk Museum boasts quite a bit of material on the Romans.

"Cairpentalloch", the town's old name, means "fort at the end of the ridge" but the Roman fort has never been certainly identified. It was probably destroyed in mediaeval times when a fortified house was erected on the site, now Peel Park. A bit of the Wall base is exposed in the north-west corner of the Park.

A convenient and good-value watering hole for

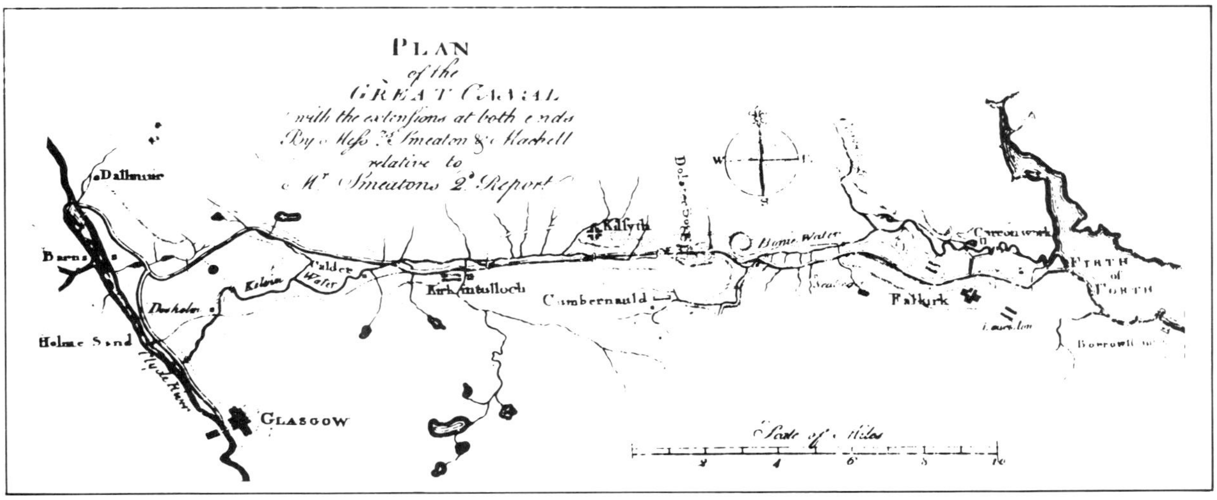

Top right: Mars, God of War, displaying Gorgon heads on his knees, originates from Balmuildy Fort. *Above:* John Smeaton's 18th-century design for the Forth and Clyde Canal. The surveyors for the Antonine Wall chose such a direct route across the Forth-Clyde isthmus, that it has been widely imitated ever since. Many roads follow this route as do 20 miles of the Forth and Clyde Canal and nine miles of the Glasgow-Edinburgh railway line.

hungry Wall walkers is the Antonine Steak House at Townhead. It used to sport a rather kitsch Roman decor but has been redecorated in an elusive Japanese style.

Altars To The Gods

There's nothing to see of either the Wall or its ditch immediately east of Kirkintilloch, but by following the A803 Kilsyth road and turning off on to the B8023 (for Twechar and Croy) you soon arrive at Auchendavy Farm, which is built slap on top of a Roman fort.

This has not been excavated for obvious reasons. However, workmen digging the Forth and Clyde Canal just behind it in 1771 found five beautiful altars and a number of other objects. Four of the altars had been put up by one man, a Roman centurion of the Second Legion called Marcus Cocceius Firmus. They are dedicated to lots of different gods, including a special spirit "that watches over the land of Britain".

The altars are all in the Hunterian Museum. So are some fascinating tombstones found at Shirva, the next farmstead along the Wall. These include one to a lady called Verecunda, probably the wife or daughter of a Roman soldier, and one to a 15-year-old boy called Salmanes. That's an unusual name for these parts and probably originates in the eastern Mediterranean. Was Salmanes the son of an eastern trader doing business with the Wall garrison or was his father serving with the Syrian archers who spent some time garrisoning Bar Hill Fort a mile to the east? It's the sort of riddle which historians love to grapple with.

These days Shirva is farmed by the Laird family. John Laird has a craggy thin face and aquiline rather Roman profile. He believes he's unlikely to find any Roman tombstones because he reckons the canal builders would have taken any flat stones when they were building the vaulted passage at the back of the farm.

Through this pend there's Twechar. It's a former mining village, as you can tell from the smoking chimneys, but there are no working pits near here any more. Twechar is one of those places that looks pretty dreary when it's dull and raining but almost attractive in the sun. It's certainly better than it was since a big park was carved out of an expanse of derelict land.

Bar Hill Treasure Trove

One of those distinctive blue Ancient Monuments signs near the War Memorial points up the farm track leading to Bar Hill Fort. Beside the track you can just make out the Antonine ditch, though it's choked with undergrowth.

At 500 feet above sea level Bar Hill is the highest fort on the Wall. In fact, from the triangulation point on the adjoining hillock, you can take in the Forth and Clyde in one panorama, weather permitting.

There's quite a lot to see at Bar Hill, which is the only fort to be set slightly back from the Wall instead of being welded on to the back of it.

The remains closest to the Wall are the bath-house. You can follow the sequence of rooms from cold to hot, though it's not so impressive as the complex at Bearsden. Up the hill a bit, the lines of the headquarters buildings are marked out. This would have been the administrative centre of the fort, where the Standards were kept under guard and the clerks maintained detailed records of every transaction.

Most impressive of all is the well, 43 feet deep, which proved to be an absolute treasure trove when it was excavated by Sir George Macdonald at the turn of the century. It was stuffed to the top with all sorts of debris: pillars, weapons, tools, ornaments and shellfish, as well as part of the winding mechanism for the well itself. The dig was paid for by Alexander Whitelaw of Gartshore, Willie Whitelaw's great uncle. He certainly got his money's worth, though he eventually gave all the finds to the Hunterian Museum.

We know from altars and inscriptions found right the way along the Wall that after Roman legionaries had finished the construction work, it was garrisoned by less valued auxiliary units, recruited originally from other parts of the Roman Empire, and composed mainly of Britons. These men weren't Roman citizens though would be granted citizenship when they were eventually discharged from their units—their children also got to be citizens but their wives didn't!

Baetasii, from the Lower Rhine, and Hamii, both Syrian archers, served at Bar Hill. The Syrians in particular must have felt they'd drawn the short straw, being sent to this wild, chilly frontier.

For the west to east traveller, who has strained both eyes and map-reading ability to stay on course so far, the next stretch is a treat. Though the Wall is no longer visible, the Antonine ditch runs away in front of you, in a deep gulley. And lifting your eyes to beyond Croy village there is the ditch again, deeply etched up the steep slope. Here, more than anywhere along the whole length of the Antonine Wall, one has the impression of the frontier of a mighty empire striking out boldly across country.

Above: *Excavated fort at Bar Hill.*

Centre spread overleaf: *Major-General William Roy, "Father of the Ordnance Survey" published his "Military Antiquities of the Romans in Britain" in 1793. It included a detailed map of the entire line of the Antonine Wall.*

THE CLYDE
Gawingburn
Old Kirkpatrick
Carlieth
Sandyford
Gateside
Inbarnet
Thornly
Laigh Longhaugh
Erskine
Erskine Kirk
Achinleek
Lawes
Burnhouse
Langfaulds
Duntocher Bridge
DUNTOCHER FORT
Achintoshin
Lawes House
Watch Hill
Dalmure
Simple house
Bargorran
L. Rossland
ROMAN CAMP
Craigton
Fontainebleau
Brewsterwells
Muir house
South Barr
Cleddin
Peel
Little Hutcheson
Braid Holm
Yealdubb
Rocket
Townend
Dum Rye
Standalon
Gardlands
Easter Drum Chapel

Muirend
French Mill
Balldarson
Upper Gavell
Ball Muley
Antermine Lock
Bear Muirs
Boghouse
Killsyth
Antermine
Kinghill
Boitfair
Over Inch Wood
Gavell
Mains of Balguharidge
House of Rinkart
Aldton
Achin Rivock
GLASSART RIV.
KELVIN RIV.
Inch Belly
Inch Brach
Inch Tarffe
Inch Lees
Twacker
Bar
Dryfield
Dykes
ACHINDAVY FORT
HILL FORT
Shelvey
Dochledge
Adamslee
THE PEEL of KIRKINTILLOCH
Solisgirth
Dumbhill
SHERVEY BURN
W. Boards
E Boards
E Garshores
Garclash
Boards Loch
Drumgrew
Townhead
Oxgang
Toddhill
Smiths
Mofs Waters
Langfold
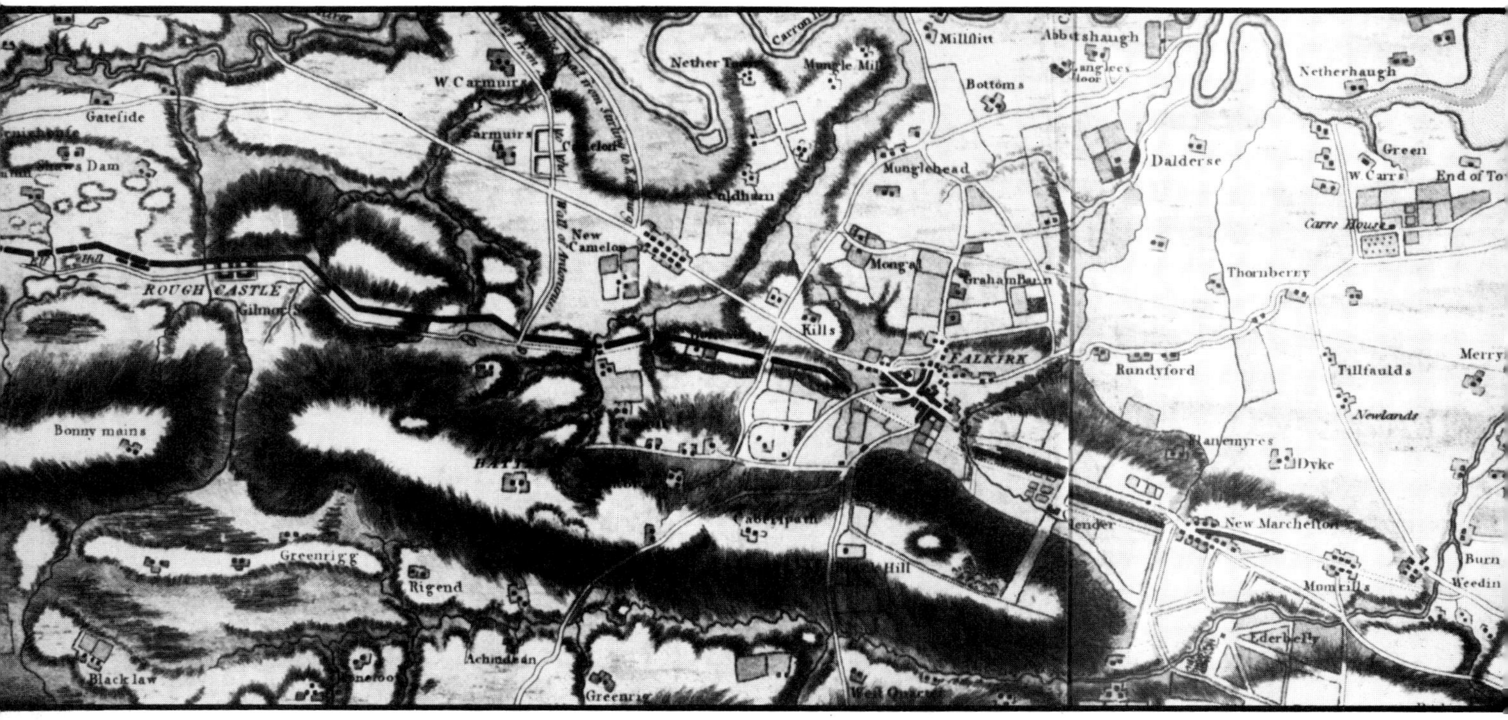
Millflitt
Abbotshaugh
Nether Tofts
Mungle Mill
Netherhaugh
W Carmuirs
Gateside
Bottoms
Carmuirs
Munglehead
Dalderse
Green
W Carrs
End of To
Carrs House
New Camelon
ROUGH CASTLE
Gilmore
Mongal
Graham Barn
Thornberry
Kills
FALKIRK
Rundyford
Tillfaulds
Newlands
Bonny mains
Dyke
New Marchelton
Greenrigg
Rigend
Hill
Burn
Weedin
Achindean
Black law
Ederbelly
Greenrig
Well Quarter

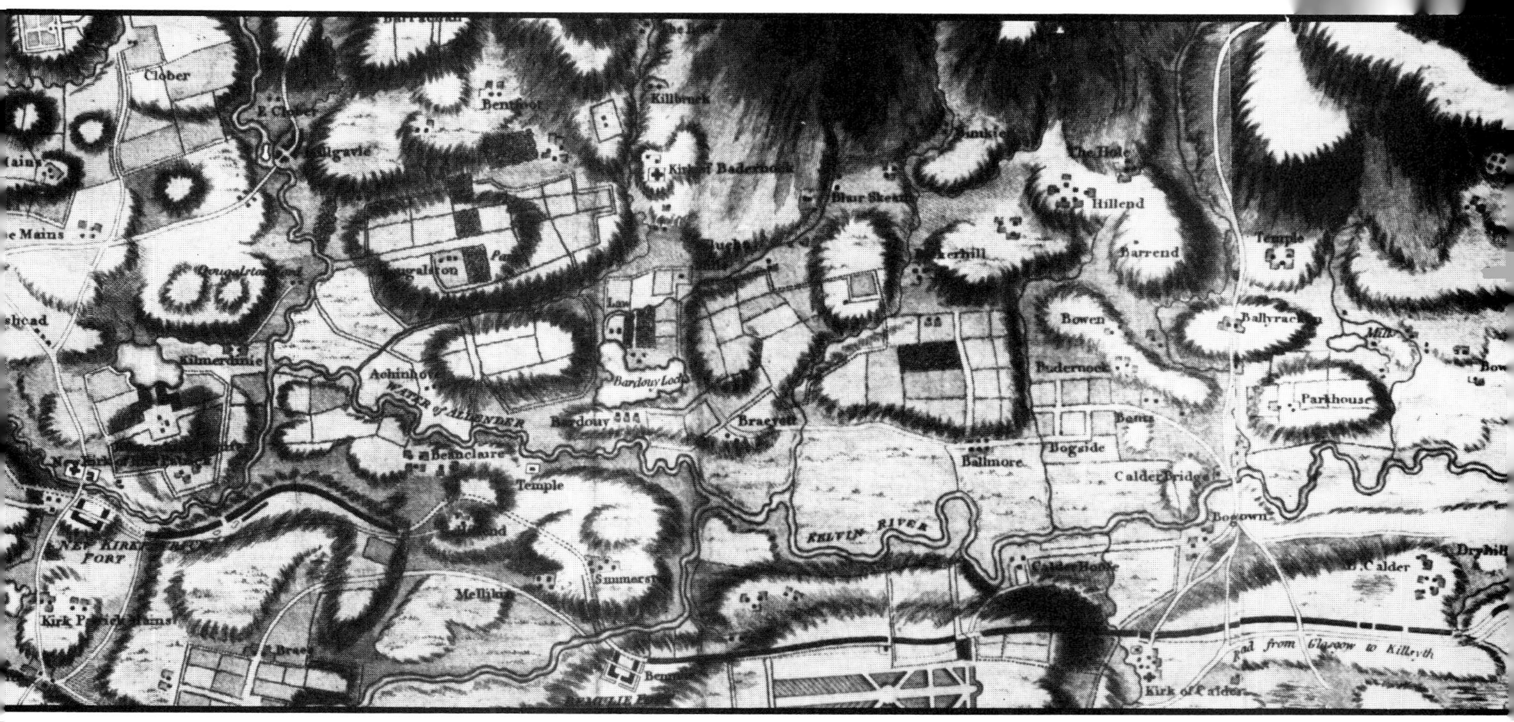

Clober
E. Clober
Kilbruck
Kirk of Badernock
Blair Skeith
The Hole
Hillend
Barrend
Temple
Bowen
Ballyracha
Badernock
Parkhouse
Mains
Mains
Kilmerdinie
WATER of ALLENDER
Bardowy Loch
Bardowy
Braeyett
Beanclaire
Temple
Ballmore
Bogside
Calder Bridge
Boghouse
NEW KIRKINTILLOCH FORT
KELVIN RIVER
Calder House
Kirk Patrick Mains
Mellikin
Summerston
Road from Glasgow to Killsyth
Kirk of Calder

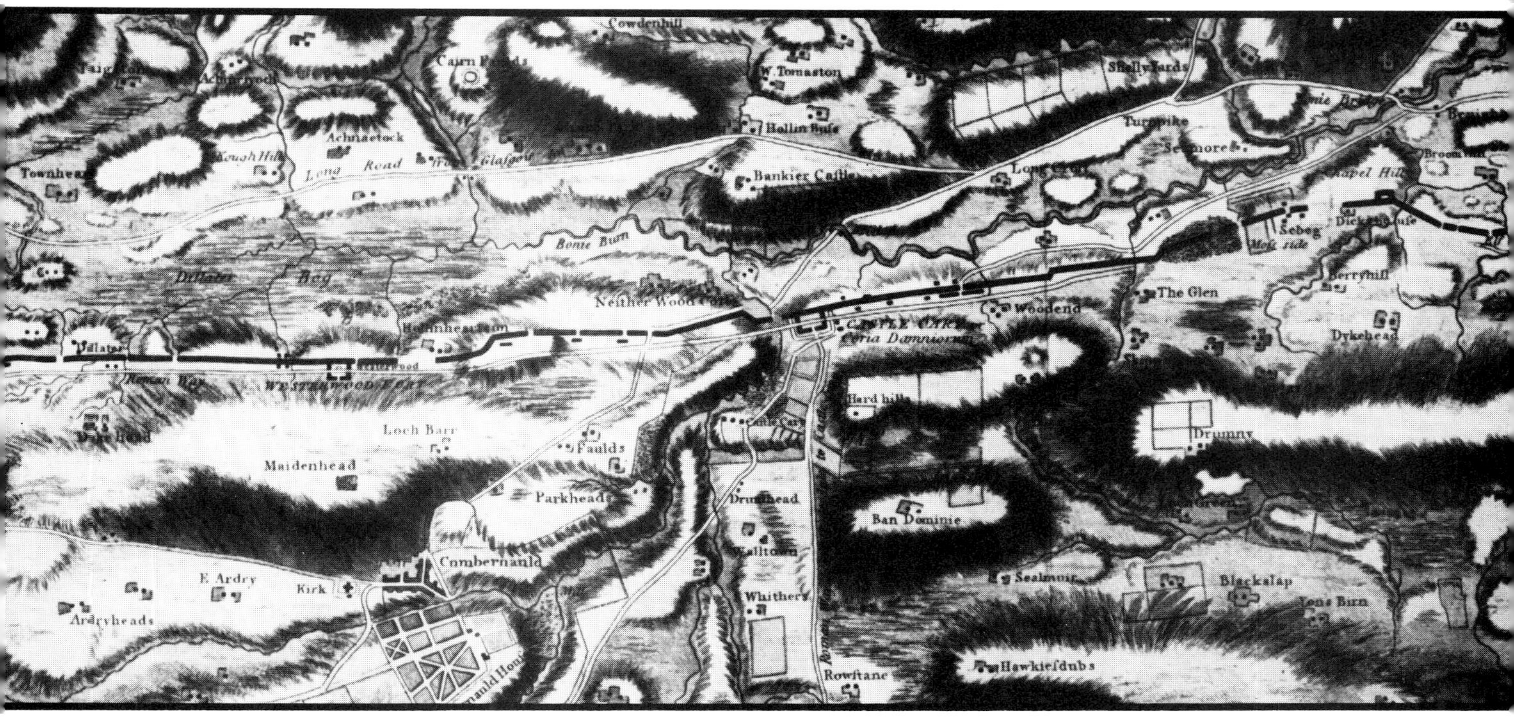

Cowdenhill
Carn Friends
W. Tonaston
Shellyards
Achineock
Achnaetock
Hollin Bus
Turnpike
Seamore
Townhead
Long Road
Bankier Castle
Chapel Hill
Bonie Burn
Dullater Bog
Sebeg
Mosside
Berryhill
Neither Wood Cote
Woodend
The Glen
CASTLE CARY
Caria Damniorum
Dykehead
Roman Way
WESTERWOOD FORT
Hard hills
Loch Barr
Faulds
Maidenhead
Drummy
Parkhead
Drumhead
Ban Dominie
Cumbernauld
E. Ardry
Kirk
Walltown
Whithers
Sealmuir
Blackslap
Ardryheads
Rowtane
Hawkiesdubs

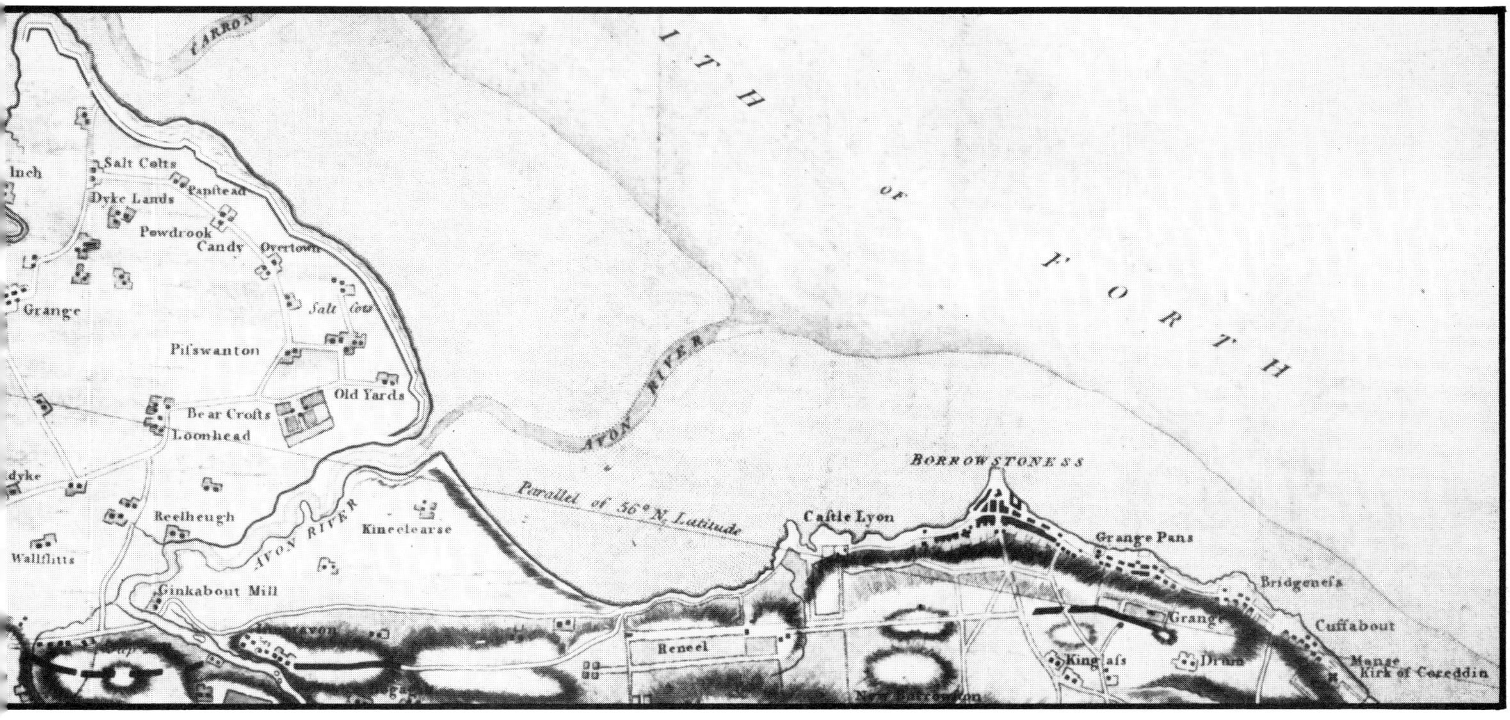

CARRON
ITH
OF
FORTH
Inch
Salt Coats
Dyke Lands
Panstead
Powdrook
Candy
Overtown
Grange
Salt Cots
Pisswanton
Old Yards
Bear Crofts
Loomhead
AVON RIVER
BORROWSTONESS
Parallel of 56° N. Latitude
Reelheugh
AVON RIVER
Kineclearse
Castle Lyon
Grange Pans
Wallflitts
Bridgeness
Ginkabout Mill
Grange
Cuffabout
Reneel
Kingass
Drum
Kirk of Coreddin

LIFE ON THE WILD FRONTIER

We have a rather stereotyped image of the Roman soldier. We imagine him to be of Italian origin, or, at least, from one of the long-established States of the Roman Empire. We think of him in armour, complete with short skirt and an iron helmet with flaps like side-burns. If we think about his everyday life, we probably imagine an almost continuous round of military exercises and encounters with the enemy, interspersed with strenuous bouts of building work.

This may all be true of the legionary soldiers who re-occupied southern Scotland on the orders of their new Emperor around 140 AD and built the Antonine Wall and its forts. But once that job was done most of them would have returned to their headquarters further south. The task of manning the Wall was then taken over by auxiliary troops. These men had been recruited to the Roman army from outlying areas of the Empire. They weren't paid as well and until they had completed their 25 years' service, they weren't even granted Roman citizenship.

We know quite a lot about the units which garrisoned the Antonine Wall from altars and dedication slabs. The First Cohort of Tungrians (from the Lower Rhine) was stationed at Castlecary, the First Cohort of Hamii (archers from Syria) helped to garrison Bar Hill and the Fourth Cohort of Gauls served at Castlehill. There was also a mounted contingent from Spain. To confuse matters further, these foreign units sometimes filled gaps in their ranks by recruiting locally. You can find in the Royal Museum of Scotland a tombstone from Mumrills to a young man called Nectovelius, who had served there with the Second Cohort of Thracians, a unit originally raised in Bulgaria. Yet the tombstone states quite clearly that Nectovelius was a Brigantian, a tribe in northern England which had once been one of the Romans' most formidable enemies.

Another misconception about the garrison is that they were constantly fighting-off attacks from the tribes living north of the Wall. A more popular view these days is that the Wall was more like a customs barrier, controlling the flow of people and goods in and out of the Roman Empire and keeping open a weather eye for trouble. If this is the case, the most formidable enemy of the men who guarded the Antonine frontier was boredom.

That is why every effort was made to keep them busy. Documents recording the daily lives of frontier soldiers come mainly from other parts of the Empire but there's no reason to think life was very different in northern Britain. Each man would

be on a rota lasting ten days or so and taking in such duties as guarding the fort gates and important buildings, cleaning weapons and uniforms, escorting important visitors and valuable consignments to other outposts, feeding and mucking-out the horses, collecting firewood and water and cleaning out the bath-house and latrines.

The forts along the Antonine Wall vary considerably in size but most share a basic lay-out to be found in forts throughout the Roman world. In the centre was the headquarters building *(principia).* The classic *principia* was a stone building with a red-tiled roof and rooms grouped around an open courtyard. This is where the clerks did their paperwork, issuing duty rosters, keeping files on each soldier, writing letters, maintaining pay records and running a savings bank.

The central room at the back of the *principia* served as a shrine. The unit's Standards were kept there, along with a statue of the Emperor. The only place on the Antonine Wall where an example can be seen is at Bar Hill, where the base of the walls has been left exposed.

The next most important building was the commanding officer's house or *praetorium.* These varied considerably in sophistication, depending on the size of the fort but were almost always stone

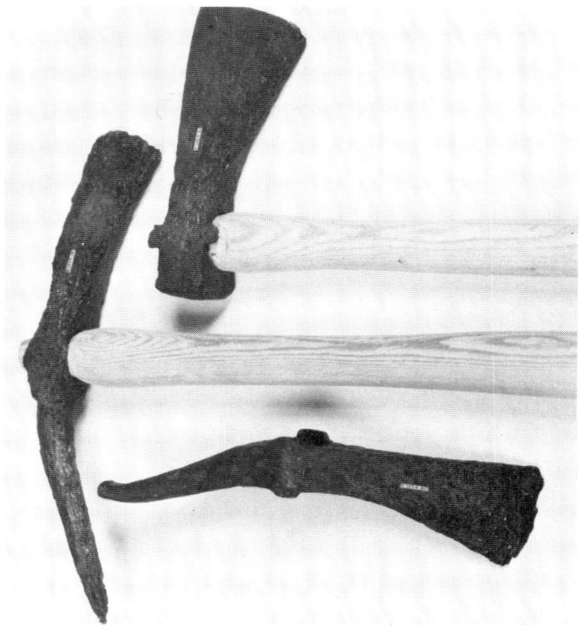

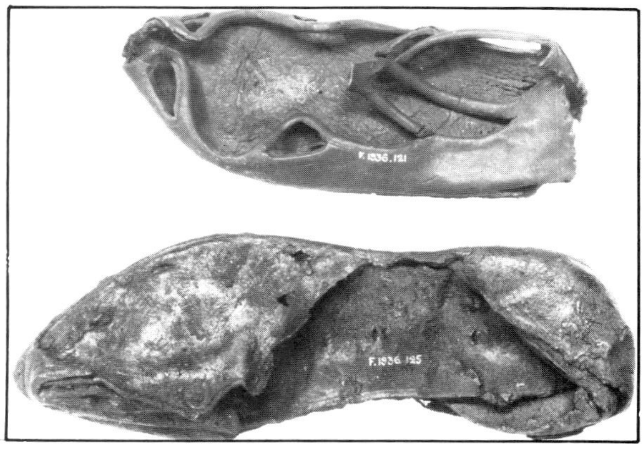

and based on the style of a Roman villa. The *praetorium* at Mumrills, the largest fort on the Wall, had its own bath-suite built into one corner. There were also remnants of red roofing tiles, window glass and a *hypocaust*, the classic Roman underfloor central heating system. The size and luxury of such buildings must have made a deep impression on natives passing through the frontier. Of course, that was part of the idea.

The third category of building that warranted an armed guard were the granaries. According to the writer Tacitus, each fort stored enough food supplies to last a year. Hence the importance of granaries which stored corn and other perishables which made up the soldier's staple diet. It has been calculated that each soldier consumed a third of a ton of corn a year. So, assuming a garrison force of 6,000 to 7,000 men, more than 2,000 tons of corn must have been stored in the granaries of the Antonine frontier forts. Provisioning of the Roman garrison must have depended on convoys of galleys arriving in harbours on the Forth and Clyde and a constant stream of wagons from the south and along the Military Way behind the Wall.

Modern day soldiers spend a lot of time thinking about their stomachs and it would be surprising if the Antonine garrison hadn't shared this great

Top left: *Auchendavy altars, including one dedicated to the "Spirit that watches over the Land of Britain".* ***Top right:*** *Tools for ditch digging.* ***Centre:*** *Well-preserved leather sandals. Both tools and sandals are now in the Hunterian Museum.* ***Above:*** *Another view of Rome's Trajan Column.*

obsession. There are no messes in Roman forts and so soldiers probably cooked and ate either in their barracks or the open air. The corn, ground down to make wholemeal bread or porridge, would have been supplemented by some meat, bought from local tribesmen or hunted down during off-duty hours. Bone remains from some forts show that beef, mutton, pork, wild boar and red deer all formed part of the diet.

However, meaty meals may have been a luxury, reserved for special festivals, because analysis of sewage deposits from the Bearsden latrines seems to point to a largely vegetarian diet including raspberries, strawberries, wild celery and hazelnuts. Also, small cheese presses have been found in some forts.

One of the commonest finds in excavations along the Wall has been fragments of amphora, which once contained oil or wine from the Mediterranean provinces. One amphora from Bar Hill has the word "vinn" stamped on the side. Wine rations were probably supplemented by locally brewed beer.

We know rather less about the auxiliary soldier's accommodation because his barracks were made of wood, probably clad in wattle and daub, and nothing remains of such structures except an arrangement of postholes. These indicate long buildings with a large room at one end for the officer in charge and a suite of smaller rooms for the rank and file. No central heating or window glass here.

The main way scholars have identified units which served time on the Antonine Wall is through the altars they set up to various deities. Those honoured include all the usual ones: Jupiter, Mars, Mercury, Apollo, Neptune, etc. But the Romans had a habit of absorbing local divinities into their worship. Thus at Bar Hill we find the commander of a unit of Syrian archers erecting an altar to Silvanus, the British woodland god. The commander of Auchendavy went so far as to dedicate an altar to "Genio Terrae Britannicae" (the Spirit that watches over the land of Britain).

The area of the soldier's existence we know the least about is his social life. We do know that Roman soldiers were not allowed to marry. But as many would have been reluctant to wait until their discharge to start a family, they often contracted unions with local women. These women, and any children they had, lived in the civil settlements *(vici)* which sprung up outside the forts. Female jewellery and women's and children's shoes found around forts back this up. The vici also provided distractions for the single man, including gambling dens, taverns and brothels. And there were shops which would have supplied some of the basic provisions for the garrison.

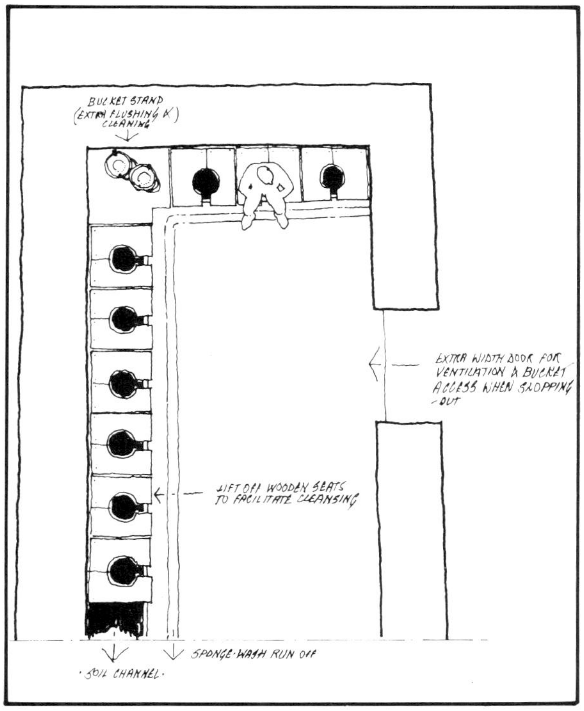

Reconstruction drawings by M. Moore. ***Top:*** *Roman bath-house.* ***Centre:*** *Latrines.* ***Above:*** *Plan of the latrines. A trip to the latrines was not the solitary pastime it is today. Excavated latrine blocks show a communal set-up with rows of wooden seats over a shallow channel, often flushed with dirty water from the bath-house. Lumps of moss or sponges on sticks were used in place of loo paper.*

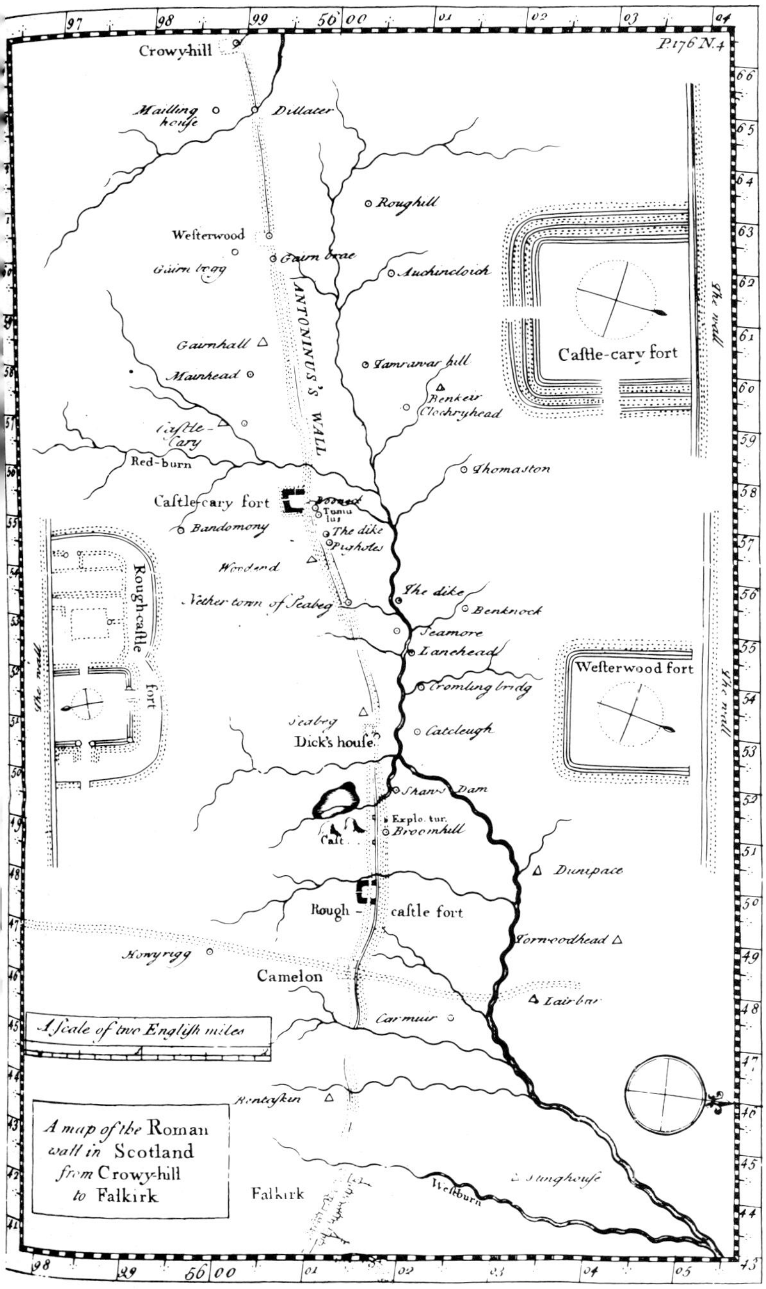

EXPLORING THE WALL

CROY TO FALKIRK

Between Croy and Castlecary the Antonine Wall neatly bisects the parliamentary constituency of Cumbernauld and Kilsyth, as it runs eastwards, shadowing the southern fringes of the Campsie Fells.

Like Twechar, the next village to the west, Croy used to be a thriving mining community but since the closure of first Bedlay and then Cardowan in 1983, there's only a handful of miners left. And for their work they have to go all the way to Fife every day. Now Croy's got the highest unemployment in the whole area and the drab council houses seem to cling desperately around the skirts of the dominating Church of the Holy Cross.

The Ancient Monuments sign is by the coal yard and just up the hill the ditch seems to double-up as a rubbish dump. It's a pity because this is one of the best preserved stretches of ditch, on account of being hewn out of solid rock, quite a job in the days before JCBs and nitro-glycerine.

There's no sign of the little fort which once crowned the top of Croy Hill, though various excavations have established its layout and finds from the site reveal a connection with the men of the Sixth Legion. From here eastwards, the best place to look for Wall finds is in the Royal Museum of Scotland in Edinburgh, successor to the National Museum of Antiquities.

The collection includes part of an intriguing stone tablet from Croy Hill. It was probably put up by soldiers of the Sixth to mark their completion of one of the fort's buildings and shows a shapely naked Venus, just out of the bath, trailing her garments and glancing alluringly behind her. Another tablet shows three legionaries; a bearded older man and two clean-shaven younger ones. They all look pretty miserable so perhaps this is the older man's tombstone and the other two figures represent his sons.

MP for Cumbernauld and Kilsyth is Norman Hogg, a big friendly man and a pretty good guide to his area. Croy Hill offers a panoramic view of just about the whole constituency. There's not much to celebrate around here: smouldering bings from now redundant pits, big factories built to house thousands of workers in the heady 60s but which are now empty or limping, Cumbernauld's last dollop of public sector housing.

But at least Cumbernauld has youth on its side. One of Scotland's five new towns, it's just 28 years old and the average age of its population is 31. And despite its employment problems it's a popular place to live.

By contrast Kilsyth, on the northern side of the Wall, has an ageing population. Inhabited since Roman times, its chief claims to fame seem to have been the Battle of Kilsyth, its religious revivals and its terrible poverty. There's a bit of an industrial estate at Queenzieburn but Norman Hogg admits: "It's disappointing that Kilsyth hasn't found new industries to replace coal and weaving."

Conspicuous Remains

Norman Hogg used to represent Bearsden but boundary changes moved him east, which gave him not only considerably more Labour votes but, as he puts it, "a much better bit of Wall".

Scholars agree. Sir George Macdonald, the great Antonine archaeologist, once remarked of the section of ditch east of Croy Hill: "Those who are able to visit the sector for themselves will need no guide, so conspicuous are the remains."

The exception is the stretch immediately beyond the fort which seems to have defeated even the Romans, such is the hardness of the rock. The 18th-century antiquary, William Maitland, was at such pains to explain this anomaly that he suggested the rock had grown since the ditch was dug! A more feasible explanation is that the escarpment is so steep in this area that a defensive ditch is really superfluous.

Opposite: *Croy Hill and its hoard.* ***Top left:*** *Three legionaries.* ***Top right:*** *Naked Venus trailing her garments.*

After around 80 feet the ditch reappears and confidently guides the explorer to Dullatur, which couldn't be more different from Croy if it tried. The first impression is of a prosperous chunk of Pollokshields transported into the middle of gently rolling countryside. There are two fine neo-classical villas designed by Alexander "Greek" Thomson and an attractive Victorian terrace.

In fact Dullatur would never have existed but for the construction of the Glasgow-Edinburgh railway line in the 1840s, which spawned Scotland's first generation of commuters. Suddenly prosperous merchants and professional men could live in the country, instead of salubrious bits of the south side and west end of Glasgow.

But no community is without its problems. While Croy folk desperately seek work, the good villagers of Dullatur complain about wild deer which invade their gardens and eat the flowers.

A familiar Ancient Monuments sign points the way up the lane leading past Dullatur Marsh, home of the redshank and jacksnipe, past plush East Dullatur House and under a railway bridge where Scotrail Express trains whoosh overhead four times an hour, forming a 90-miles-per-hour link between Scotland's first and second cities.

Beyond the bridge the now familiar hollow of the Antonine ditch reappears like a faithful retainer and leads the way to the site of Westerwood Fort. There's an old farm in one corner which has been turned into the Westerwood Jubilee Youth Centre, opened by Prince Charles in 1980. Every weekend lots of boys and girls pack in for all sorts of open air activities like rock climbing and wind surfing.

The Centre stands in the north-west angle of a small Roman fort. You can just about trace the ditches. Though it was excavated in the 1930s, only bits of stone buildings have been uncovered—one was probably in the bath-house.

Wall explorers. ***Top left:*** *Anne Johnstone with Norman Hogg.* ***Top right:*** *The Antonine Wall at Seabegs.* ***Above:*** *Aerial view of Rough Castle Fort and the Wall showing the "lilia" to the right of the ditch.*

East of Westerwood the Wall is conveniently marked by a splendid line of mature oaks and beeches along the crest of the ridge, though there are lots of fences to climb. This stretch is more an obstacle course than a detective trail.

The ditch, now just a shallow hollow, continues past the demolished farmstead of Garnhall, nice and handy to the cosy bar of Castlecary House Hotel which offers hot drinks and meals as well as the usual liquid refreshments.

Castlecary is slashed through one way by the Glasgow-Edinburgh rail line and the other by the Glasgow-Stirling motorway. That's been bad news for the Antonine Wall and even worse for the fort there, the only one with stone walls apart from Balmuildy. Stones from the ramparts had already been robbed to build both the Livingston family's nearby tower-house in the 1470s and the Forth and Clyde Canal, which has shadowed the Wall ever since Kirkintilloch. The railway builders trumped this double dose of vandalism in 1840 by cutting right across the fort. Today observant commuters can glimpse momentarily the site of the main buildings among a clump of trees.

Castlecary has produced a great harvest of finds, including the mouthpiece for a brass instrument of some kind and an altar to Neptune, set up by the First Cohort of Vardullians, a mounted contingent originally raised in Spain.

We're now out of Strathclyde and into Central Region, whose planners are keen to publicise "their bit" of the Antonine Wall. So far their hopes of creating a signed walkway between Castlecary and Falkirk have been frustrated. However, there is a

Top: *Excavation at Rough Castle Fort, 1904, and,* ***Centre:*** *At the same spot in 1985, the modern-day Wall garrison.* ***Above:*** *The Wall and ditch approaching Rough Castle from Bonnybridge.*

modest scheme to provide information about both the Wall and the Forth and Clyde Canal at the new car park built to serve the old loch-house at Underwood, which is being converted into a pub and restaurant.

A few hundred yards down the road is Seabegs Wood. In the midst of a rather tatty rundown landscape, this stretch of the Antonine frontier has somehow retained a powerful ancient feel to it. From the site of a recently discovered fortlet at the eastern boundary the rampart and ditch strike away through a thinly wooded area of oak, birch and holly, a habitat probably quite similar to what the Romans found here in the Second Century.

At the south side of the wood lies perhaps the best surviving stretch of the Military Way, the road which ran parallel to the Wall. It's cobbled surface is now grassed over but there's no mistaking the line of it.

Signs of the ditch peter out in the western outskirts of Bonnybridge. It can be picked up again by following a lane beside the former Smith and Wellstood factory, where wonderful curly cast iron stoves used to come from.

Considering The Lilies

East to Rough Castle Fort you can follow the ditch, first as a shallow congested hollow, then a deep gulley, with the Wall quite recognisable on the southern side. Rough Castle may be the second smallest fort on the Wall (only one acre) but it's by far the best preserved. For once little imagination is needed. You can follow the ramparts and ditches all the way round before leaving by the auspicious north gate to inspect the "lilies", a honeycomb of amazing defensive pits, which would have been filled with sharp stakes camouflaged by twigs and leaves. Designed to confuse the enemy, they can still trap the unwary.

Today the Wall's enemies don't need to creep up on it in the night. They can just walk in. Part of the Rough Castle rampart has evidently been used for motorbike scrambling and explanatory notices are sometimes peppered with air gun shot.

Against the massed ranks of destruction stands the Antonine Wall squad. There are only seven of them, plus a chargehand and a superintendent. They're employed by Historic Buildings and

Monuments and they look after the bits of Wall which are in the "care of the Secretary of State".

The phrase may make it sound as if Scotland's Number One MP personally picks up the rubbish and keeps the grass short but really he pays a rather pathetic salary to men like Archie Ferguson to do it for him.

Archie's retired now and living just south of the Wall near Falkirk but can't resist popping back regularly to see how "his boys" are getting on. He started working on the Antonine Wall in 1952. "I'd got a job with what used to be the Ministry of Works. They said it would last about six weeks."

Well, more than 30 years later, he was still at it, issuing forth each morning with his little posse in an Ancient Monuments van to tend bits of the Antonine frontier all the way from Bearsden to Falkirk. Historic Buildings and Monuments is responsible for 130 acres of the Wall altogether and it was Archie's job to keep them smart and Bristol fashion and help out archaeologists with the heavy work.

He did the job so well and so cheerfully that he now boasts a chestful of official gongs—the Silver Jubilee Medal, the BEM and the Imperial Service Medal.

If there's one thing that really gets his goat it's litter bugs. Litter bugs love ditches and the Antonine ditch is just perfect for them. "You tell the police but it's hopeless. They say you've got to catch them at it," said Archie.

East of Rough Castle, beyond a sordid industrial wasteland where a guano factory adds a distinctive aroma, there's a good section of ditch, absolutely choked with rubbish, especially near the Ancient Monuments sign saying "No dumping by order".

Amidst all this chaos there's a little patch of neatness called "Tayavalla". It's a concoction of Gaelic and Latin meaning "the House on the Wall" and Fred Harvey lives there. The ditch in his garden is so deep he has a little wooden bridge to reach his back lawn. In the summer he grows peas and potatoes in the ditch but says it's too shady for anything else. He seems happy to chat to Wall explorers but reckons barely 20 have called in the 30 years he's been there.

A few hundred yards along Tamfourhill Road lies Watling Lodge. There, running through a public park like a great chasm, is the best surviving stretch of ditch. Along most of the frontier a build-up of earth and debris has reduced the ditch to at best a shallow hollow. But at Watling Lodge it retains its original profile, a distinctive V-shape and, at 40 feet wide by more than 12 feet deep, must have more or less kept its original dimensions too.

Here more than anywhere you realise the enormity of the task which faced the soldiers of the three Roman legions who built the Wall, probably in a mere two or three years. And here you understand the awe the Antonine Wall instilled in anyone approaching this outpost of the Roman Empire.

***Top:** Rough Castle "lilia" excavated in 1904, and, **Opposite:** The same site today. **Above:** Wall explorers at Watling Lodge.*

THE LIGHT THE SPADE HAS BROUGHT

"There are occasions when doubt and uncertainty inevitably remain, were it not for the light that the spade has brought." The subject of this observation is the Antonine Wall and the writer is Sir George Macdonald, the best known and most controversial of the Wall's archaeologists.

Though essentially an amateur, Macdonald's excavations, spanning more than 30 years up to his death in 1949, and his magnum opus, *The Roman Wall in Scotland* (1934), continue to have enormous influence on practically everything said or written about the Antonine frontier. The study of the Wall still tends to be seen as pre- or post- Macdonald.

Until almost into this century consideration of the Wall had been mostly in terms of its visible remains. In the description of the Wall from Aberdonian, Alexander Gordon, we can see the germ of an archaeological method. He walked the frontier from west to east in 1725, measuring its dimensions at frequent intervals (not always accurately). He also discovered the Wall had a stone foundation.

And in 1775 Major-General William Roy, founding father of the Ordnance Survey, made a complete survey of it, which was so good that archaeologists still find his map a handy reference, especially in areas which have since been built over.

At the same time nobody had considered excavation as a way of expanding knowledge about the Wall's purpose, construction and the way of life of its garrison.

Sometimes labourers would stumble on remains, as when a Roman bath-house at Ferrydyke in Old Kilpatrick was accidently uncovered in 1790 during the construction of the Forth and Clyde Canal. A delightfully ungrammatical manuscript by a contemporary, John Millar Morison, describes the discovery of "A subteraneous Building surrounded with A wall Built with freestone and Lime", together with many silver coins.

"Mr John Clerk overseer of the Clyde has told me since that him and some of the boys in Kilpatrick went to the place after the men had give over work and Diged and got a good many of them (coins)."

A number of other items were unearthed along other sections of the Canal, which follows the line of the wall for 20 miles, and in the 1840s more came to light during the construction of the Glasgow-Edinburgh railway line. Some of the material thrown up by these haphazard excavations have since found their way into the Royal Museum of Scotland and the Hunterian Museum at Glasgow University. How many more, one wonders, disappeared into the homes of local landowners and the pockets of labourers, or were simply discarded as worthless? Moreover, as nobody logged what had been found and where, the sections of the frontier destroyed by these great engineering projects are lost to us for ever. More were or would be obliterated by ploughing and house building.

The first systematic attempt to investigate the remains was made in the 1890s by the Glasgow Archaeological Society. A series of excavations established the basic structure of the Wall ditch and Military Way.

But there's no doubt that the individual who has had most impact on the study of the Antonine Wall is Sir George Macdonald. Though once a Classics lecturer, in 1903 he went to work for the Scottish Education Department and eventually became its Secretary. In fact, his knighthood was for services to education. Nevertheless his first love was the Antonine Wall, which he refers to as "the Limes", from the Latin word for "boundary". His work on it included a string of major excavations and literally scores of trial trenches. It was largely a single-handed effort, often with Macdonald in great coat and fedora supervising just one trained workman.

His most productive major excavation was his first, starting in 1902, at Bar Hill, the highest fort on the Wall, commanding a magnificent view of the Forth-Clyde nexus. It is slightly set back from the Wall and, as Macdonald discovered, appears to have been built on top of another fort. Recent excavations suggest that it is Antonine.

In the *principia*, or main administrative building, he identified the *sacellum*, the inner sanctum where the Standards were kept, and an open courtyard. In the courtyard was a well. "The discovery and clearance of this supplied the most exciting episode of the excavations."

In fact, it is probably the richest cache of Antonine material ever found in Scotland. "When the fort was abandoned," writes Macdonald, "the water-supply had been effectively cut off by choking the well with a mass of the most miscellaneous material, including besides many building-stones, a large altar bearing an inscription, three fragments of an inscribed slab and as many as 21 freestone columns."

Mixed with the masonry were parts of the well-bucket and pulley, a mass of leather articles, including children's shoes, iron weapons and tools, animal bones, shells and coins, all important clues about the life of the fort's garrison.

Macdonald continued to dig throughout the First World War, writing to a friend that he was "toiling away at the Wall but with little sustained time."

The imposing portrait of Macdonald in the National Portrtait Gallery in Edinburgh brings to mind an Old Testament patriach. He certainly had an imperious manner and was reputed to be a brute to work for. Something of this is conveyed by a

Opposite: *Sir George Macdonald, "Dracula-like" in a trench at Mumrills.*

photograph of him in the 1920's, staring fiercely from the bottom of a trench at Mumrills and looking a bit like Dracula about to rise from the grave.

There's also a certain arrogance of tone in his prodigious writing about the Wall which has tended to stifle debate. New scientific methods have liberated scholars to challenge some of Macdonald's assumptions, but only recently.

For example, Macdonald assumed that the construction of the Antonine frontier was part of a great blueprint, with the locations of the forts all planned beforehand. But it now seems more likely that only half a dozen or so forts were planned, which would have been interspersed with fortlets. The recent discovery of a number of these fortlets by Lawrence Keppie and others supports this idea.

And, although Macdonald found animal bones and shellfish debris at Bar Hill, the analysis of sewage deposits from the latrine block at Bearsden, excavated by David Breeze, indicates a largely vegetarian diet.

A fresh crop of evidence has come from new techniques, like aerial photography. Also, modern archaeologists have evolved better methods of tracing the remains of timber buildings and pay more attention to the civil settlements which seem to have sprung up around some forts.

In 1985 an excavation under Geoff Bailey of Falkirk Museums challenged one of Macdonald's most fundamental assumptions: that the Wall started at Bridgeness, close to the spot where the magnificent Bridgeness Slab was discovered in 1868 by local historian, Henry Cadell.

In advance of a housing development in the area by Mr Cadell's grandson, William Cadell, Bailey dug a series of trial trenches over the site and found no evidence whatsoever of Roman occupation. Perhaps the Wall didn't finish here after all but at Carriden, the Roman fort a mile further east. Nobody's hanging his hat on the new theory, not yet. It still presents problems, like how this very heavy slab got all the way from Carriden to Bridgeness.

There's plenty more to be found out about the Antonine Wall from archaeology. Three forts,

Carriden, Auchendavy and Castlehill have never been excavated. They are being left for future generations and more refined scientific methods.

Besides, there aren't many Roman archaeologists in Scotland and most of them are kept pretty busy with "rescue work"—that's investigating an area which is about to be obliterated by development. Even with legislation to protect most of the frontier, there are likely to be 20 or 30 threats to different bits of it at any one time.

After an excavation, it is now customary for archaeologists to fill in the remains they have uncovered. This is to protect them from the combined assault of weather and vandalism. The only exceptions, apart from a few short stretches of Wall base, are the outlines of the fortlet at Kinneil Park, the headquarters building and bath-house at Bar Hill and the bath-house at Bearsden.

There might be more interest in the Antonine Wall if there was more to see. Most people find it hard to recreate in their imaginations the Roman occupation of Scotland from grassy humps and hollows or even the consolidated foundations of a building. Perhaps the most crying need just now is not for more archaeology but facilities to help the general public appreciate what has been discovered so far.

An interpretative centre, using good graphics and reproductions, somewhere along the line of the Wall, would be a start. It would act as a launching pad to propel inquirers towards the best bits of the remains and the finest museum collections. Better still perhaps would be a full-scale mock-up of one of the smaller forts or part of the Wall, as at Vindolanda, the civilian settlement near Hadrian's Wall.

There must be something lacking when Scottish schoolchildren who have never seen the Antonine Wall are regularly bussed to Northumberland to help them make that imaginative leap back to Roman times.

Excavations at Rough Castle, 1904. ***Above:*** *Excavations at Mumrills. Sir George Macdonald and his team of archaeologists.*

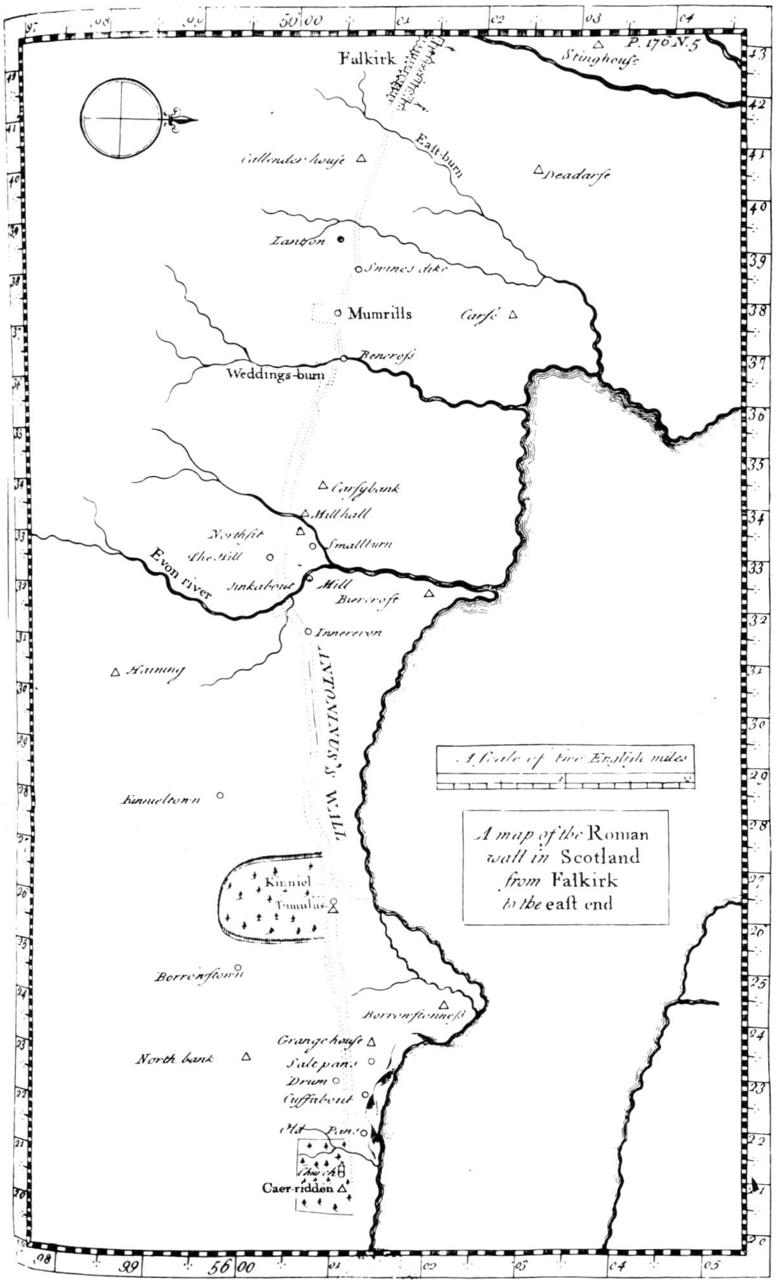

EXPLORING THE WALL
FALKIRK TO THE FORTH

"Something there is that doesn't want a wall, that wants it down."

Robert Frost.

That certainly applies to the Antonine Wall and its accompanying ditch. And it's not just the ravages of time and decay that are responsible for obliterating so much of it. Many of those who operate on or near the Wall seem to have regarded it as a nuisance rather than an asset.

The Wall is no sooner out of the protective guardianship of the Secretary of State at Watling Lodge, than there's Barr's soft drinks factory plonked on top of it. Thereafter it's almost swallowed by modern Falkirk, apart from a length of ditch within the horseshoe shape of Anson Avenue in Bantaskin, where it's marked by a line of beech trees.

Then it crosses the charmingly named Maggie Wood's Loan, where the Hanoverian cannons got stuck in the mud, prior to the second Battle of Falkirk, the rather lucky Jacobite victory of 1746. The Wall route continues eastwards along what is now Arnothill Lane into the area known as Pleasance which is long thought to have contained a Roman fort.

We'll probably never know now as the area is swallowed by building, though a bit further east in the car park in Kemper Avenue, Glasgow University's 'Wall buff', Lawrence Keppie, uncovered the foundations of a Roman building in 1980. It had underfloor central heating and was probably a bath-house or part of an inn for Roman travellers.

From here the Wall line strikes off between some blocks of flats, one of the most salubrious municipal highrise developments in Britain, on the edge of Callendar Park.

The Forbes family used to own this area. Today the grounds are a strikingly beautiful public park, complete with boating lake and exotic woodland, though the house itself, now owned by the District Council, has been empty for some time.

Along the north edge of the park you can follow a well preserved stretch of ditch, ten feet deep in places, until you come in line with the house, where there's a great bite missing.

The details of the story are a bit vague but one version has it that William Forbes ordered it to be cut so that Queen Victoria would get a good view of his splendid pile as she passed in her carriage. But his vanity was in vain because she was looking the other way at the time.

There is also the story of an unfortunate amateur archaeologist who got arrested as a spy when exploring this section of the Roman frontier during the First World War.

The ditch disappears into the private grounds of Callendar Park College of Education, re-emerging beyond a railway bridge in Grahamsdyke Street. "Grahamsdyke" is the old name for the Antonine Wall and it survives in place names all along its route. Legend has it that this name comes from a native British hero, called Gryme, who eventually overthrew the Romans and destroyed the Wall but Dr Keppie thinks there's a more prosaic explanation. "Gryme means strong and a dyke is a wall, so it simply means strong wall," he says.

Tungri and Thracians at Mumrills

Just along the road at Sandy Loan is the site of Mumrills Fort. It covers more than six acres, making it the biggest fort on the Wall. There's no trace of it today, though Sir George Macdonald excavated here in the 1920s. He located a group of stone buildings in the centre, including a much rebuilt *principia* or HQ, where all administrative work went on and the Standards were housed. He also found two granaries and a particularly impressive *praetorium* or commanding officer's house, complete with its own bath suite. He traced streets, laid out in the usual grid pattern, and found the rest of the site pock-marked with postholes, indicating the long, thatched, wattle and daub spartan barracks, used by the garrison troops.

A tombstone and an altar found locally indicate the presence of two units. First on the scene was probably the prestigious cavalry regiment of Tungri, originally from the Lower Rhine, perhaps the only purely cavalry regiment to have manned the Wall. Next came a mixed foot and mounted cohort of Thracians recruited from Greece. Each would have been 500 strong.

They left behind them lots of bits and pieces which have since found their way into the Royal Museum of Scotland, including a ladle, a military belt fitting and large flanged tiles which would have covered the bath-house and headquarters buildings.

East of Mumrills the line of the Wall is completely obliterated by the M9 Edinburgh-Stirling Motorway but it re-emerges at Polmont Old Parish Church. The church itself is Victorian but in the churchyard there are some spine-chilling older tombstones, bearing skulls and hourglasses.

Next stop is Millhall Wood where there's a good length of ditch, though few people know about it and fewer get round to visiting it. Then it disappears into Grangemouth Golf Course. The next recognisable bit of ditch runs down a slope to the road beyond the clubhouse. The Wall itself is skirted by a council-owned artificial ski slope—another example of a curious planning decision.

Soon after this the walker is brought to an abrupt halt by the River Avon, which is a bit deep to ford under normal circumstances. Did the Romans build a bridge here and was the Wall built across the river? Some worked stones on the river bed indicate that there might have been a bridge, though maybe this was for travellers along the Military Way behind the Wall. After all, it's hard to imagine a turf wall being built on a bridge over a river.

The modern Wall-traveller is forced to make a quick detour to the road-bridge downstream. The little side road, marked for Inveravon and Upper Kinneil gets you back on course. The rise on the east bank of the river looks just the spot for a fort and walls have been found here, as well as bits of tiles and pottery.

Well into this century a bit of the Military Way was used by the farmer at Inveravon (beside an old ruined tower), but apparently the cows kept getting their hoofs caught between the stones so he cleared it away.

When Romans Ruled

The Wall more or less follows the road eastwards from here, emerging on the top of a long ridge. On a fine day this offers an exhilarating panorama of the Forth. Beyond it rises the Kingdom of Fife and the Ochil Hills, while in the foreground the nine great cooling towers and pencil-thin flare stacks of the Grangemouth petro-chemical complex can look curiously clean and new in bright sunshine. Note also the raised beach, where the remains of prehistoric barbecues have been found.

The view across the Forth is a reminder of Roman rule north of the river, focused on Ardoch, Strageath and Bertha, the string of forts stretching up to the River Tay. Dr David Breeze of the Ancient Monuments Inspectorate says that people have tended to assume that there were as yet undiscovered forts at Seabegs, Falkirk and Kinneil, mirroring the spacing of forts in the western section of the frontier. "There's little hard evidence to support this. It could be that the eastern section of the Wall relied for its protection on the forts extending north-east into Perthshire."

Past Nether Kinneil, across a field and through a little conifer wood, the Wall emerges in Kinneil Park, a favourite spot for local leg stretching. A Roman fortlet was discovered at the western end of the park in 1978 after Antonine pottery had been turned up during ploughing in the area. Part of it has been left exposed and there's a good information board. These miniature forts helped plug the gaps between the proper forts but they offered little comfort. No bath-house here, just a couple of wooden shacks to shelter the patrols.

There's no sign of the Wall itself at this point but the ditch runs on across the park as a gentle hollow towards Kinneil House which is built over the

The magnificent Bridgeness Slab, now in the Royal Museum of Scotland, once marked the eastern terminal of the Antonine Wall.

northern lip of the ditch and has subsided as a consequence.

Falkirk District Council have taken over the coachhouse and turned it into a lively little museum (closed in winter), with a good section on the Antonine Wall. Their most impressive exhibit is the altar to the nymphs of the woods and cross-roads, erected by Vibia Pacata, wife of the centurion commanding Westerwood Fort near Castlecary. The museum also gives a summary of the history of the surrounding area. Even not counting the Antonine Wall, there's lots of it.

In Kinneil Estate alone there were Mesolithic remains, a 9th-century rune stone, a 12th-century church (part still standing), a deserted mediaeval village and the House itself, which probably dates back to the 13th century. In one of its outhouses James Watt experimented with steam engines when he was a guest of Dr James Roebuck, founder of Falkirk's late lamented Carron Company. Roebuck was looking for a pump to take water from the coalmine he'd had dug at Kinneil, also recently closed.

The Wall's Eastern End

A big question mark hangs over the eastern terminus of the Wall. It must be on the Forth somewhere near here but where exactly?

It has generally been assumed that it was obliterated by the modern town of Bo'ness. Maps show the probable route as along Dean Road, Grahamsdyke Road and Grahamsdyke Lane, ending somewhere around Harbour Road near Bridgeness Tower, which was built to guard against a French invasion.

This theory is largely based on the discovery in 1868 of an impressive distance slab erected by a squad from the Second Legion.

It depicts a macho Roman cavalryman riding-down four naked and pathetic-looking natives and a victory celebration service with a pig, a ram and a bull, waiting to be sacrificed. Really subtle stuff, this Roman propaganda. The original is in the Royal Museum of Scotland, though the inscription is reproduced on a worn wall plaque in Harbour Road, hopefully soon to be replaced.

It reads: "For the Emperor Titus Aelius Hadrianus Antoninus Augustus Pius, Father of his country, the Second Augustan Legion completed the work for 4652 paces."

This is thought to refer to the section of Wall between Bridgeness and Inveravon. However, a recent excavation failed to turn up any trace of Roman occupation at Bridgeness. One possibility is that the Wall didn't end in Bo'ness at all but at the Roman fort at Carriden three-quarters of a mile away. But that leaves the problem of the 4652 paces. To get from Inveravon to Carriden in 4652 paces whoever did the measuring must have been taking pretty big steps! In the absence of conclusive evidence archaeologists will continue to argue the toss.

Maybe that's the most exciting thing about the Antonine Wall. It's a detective trail which yields lots of clues but doesn't give up its secrets without a struggle. After nearly two millennia this enduring monument to Roman engineering and thwarted ambition is still keeping us guessing.

The discovery of the Bridgeness Slab is described in the diary of Henry Cadell which is now in the possession of his grandson, William Cadell. This photograph shows the gardener at Grange behind the newly discovered slab. It was unearthed in three pieces by "a man, wishing to enlarge his kailyard" in April 1868, and taken to Grange where it remained until it was presented to the National Museum of Antiquities in February 1869.

"WELL I NEVER . . ."

Did The North Britons Fight Naked?

Several of the Distance Slabs found along the Antonine Wall depict native warriors, either as bound captives or being thoroughly outclassed in battle by Roman cavalry. Most of these warriors are shown either naked or wearing only a loin cloth. Did they fight naked or are they just shown that way to exaggerate their helplessness? Some native chain mail has been found by archaeologists in England. On the other hand, literary sources speak of them eschewing body-armour. The third-century writer, Dio Cassius, describes the natives as living in tents, "unclothed and unshod, sharing their women and bringing up all their children together". Mind you, some of the claims he makes on their behalf rather strain one's credulity. They could hold out for many days he says, by plunging into marshes, with only their heads above water!

General Pitt-Rivers, 1894, the first inspector of Ancient Monuments, in a letter to Glasgow Archaeological Society: "This work is not a mere Scotch monument; it is even more than a National Monument. Being the most northerly boundary of the Roman Empire, it is of interest to the whole civilised world, and the nation that allows the last vestige of such work to perish will stand badly by the side of others that take a more enlightened view of such matters."

Windows

In all the Antonine Wall forts excavated so far, fragments of window glass have been found, though this luxury would have been restricted to the main buildings, and metal grills more commonly used. We don't know the size of the panes, or how they were made. They may have been cast in moulds, or they might have been blown into a cylinder which was then cut open and flattened out. Some sort of cement would have held them in place.

Leonard Cottrell, 1967, writer on archaeology: "Stretches of the Antonine Wall still remain, and though they lack the lonely magnificence of Hadrian's monument, they have a different type of appeal. Unlike the Northumbrian Wall, which runs mainly through unfrequented country, parts of the Antonine rampart now keep company with factories, golf courses, suburban gardens and other evidence of Scotland's more recent history. Oddly enough, these do not detract from its fascination; in some ways they increase it."

Many A Slip

Even legionary stonemasons made mistakes sometimes. For instance, a Second Legion distance slab found near Balmuildy contains the word *pep* instead of *per* (Latin for "over a distance of").

Lawrence Keppie, 1985, curator at the Hunterian Museum, Glasgow University: "Most people don't realise the Romans got this far. In England they tend to assume that the invasion stopped at Hadrian's Wall. But in some ways the Antonine Wall is more exciting. Just think of it as a detective trail."

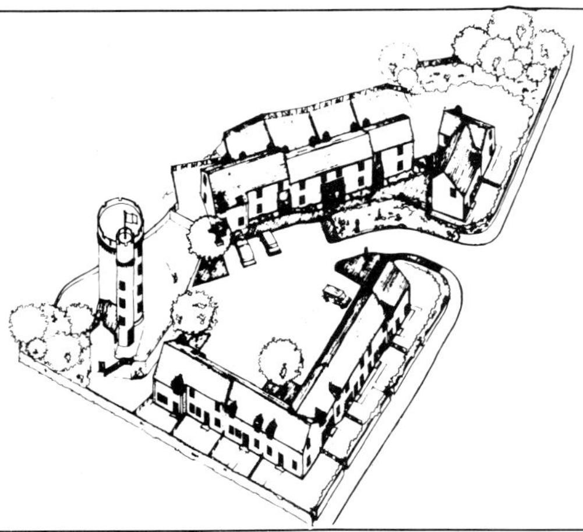